PICTURE BOOK OF
FOOD

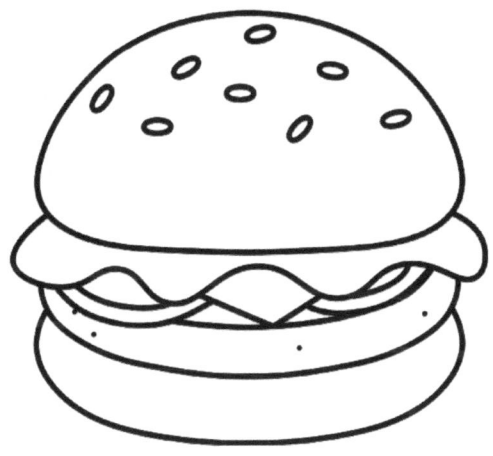

...By...
Ella Caldwell

Copyright © 2024. All rights reserved.

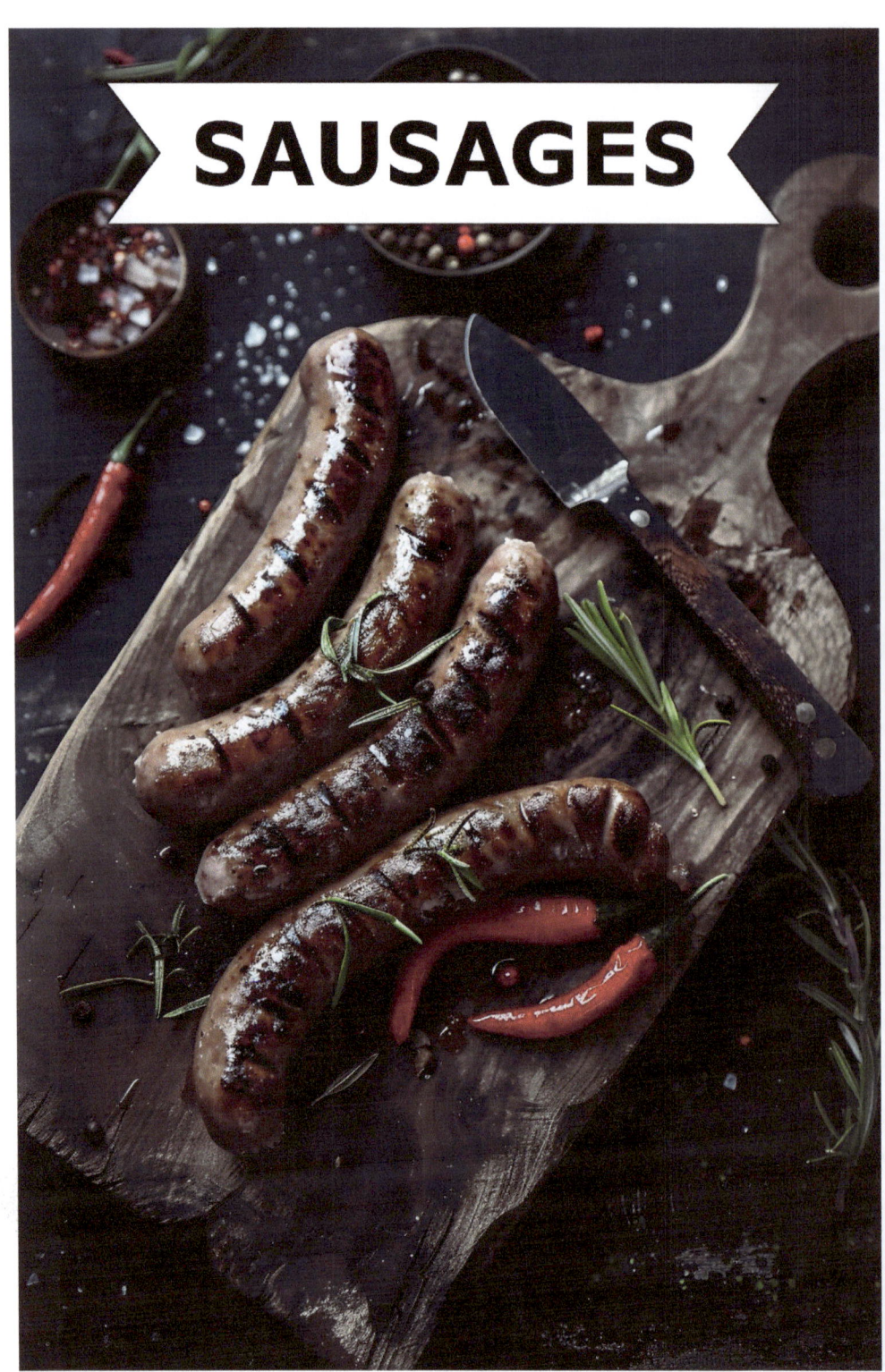

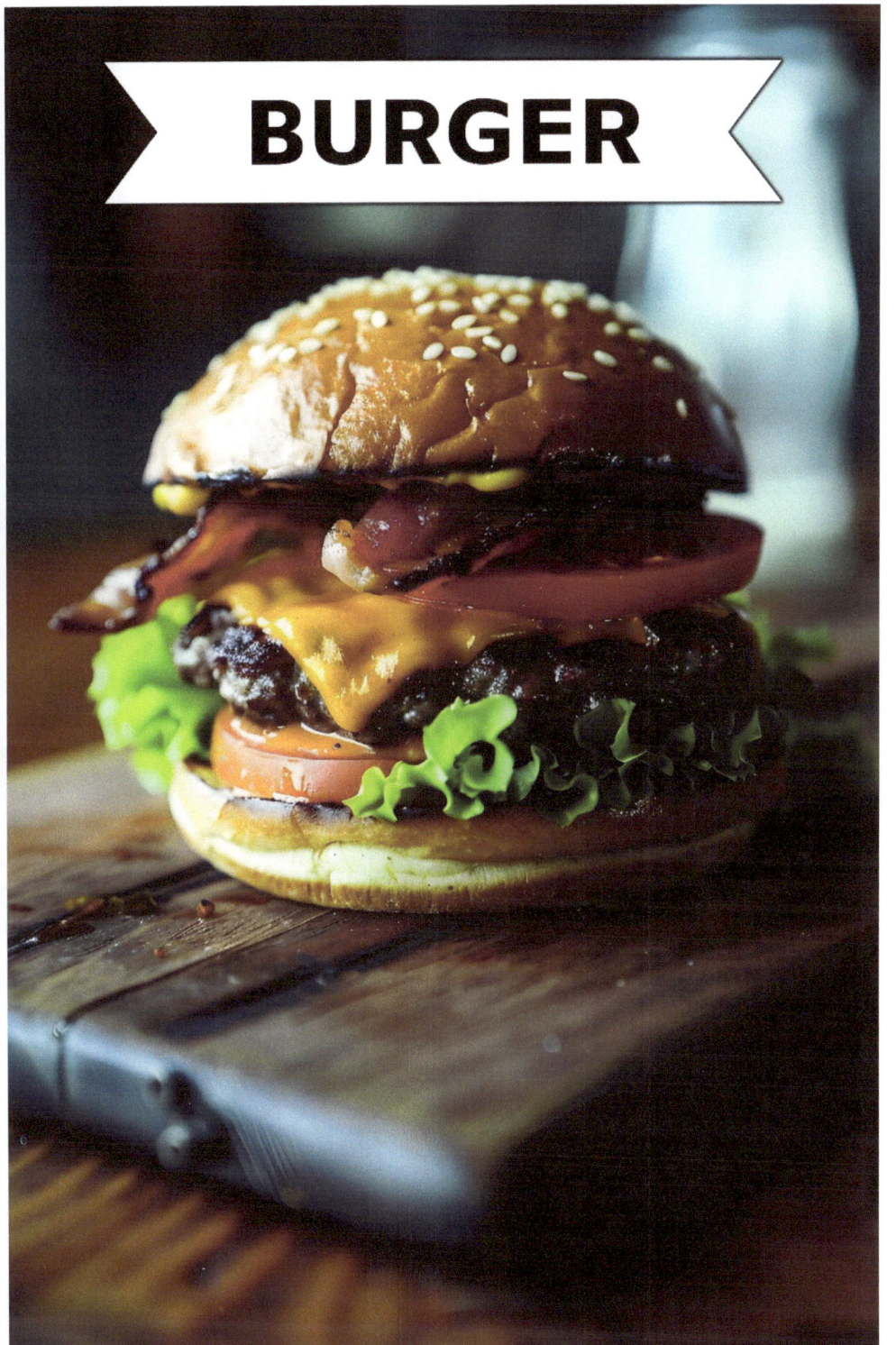

PIZZA

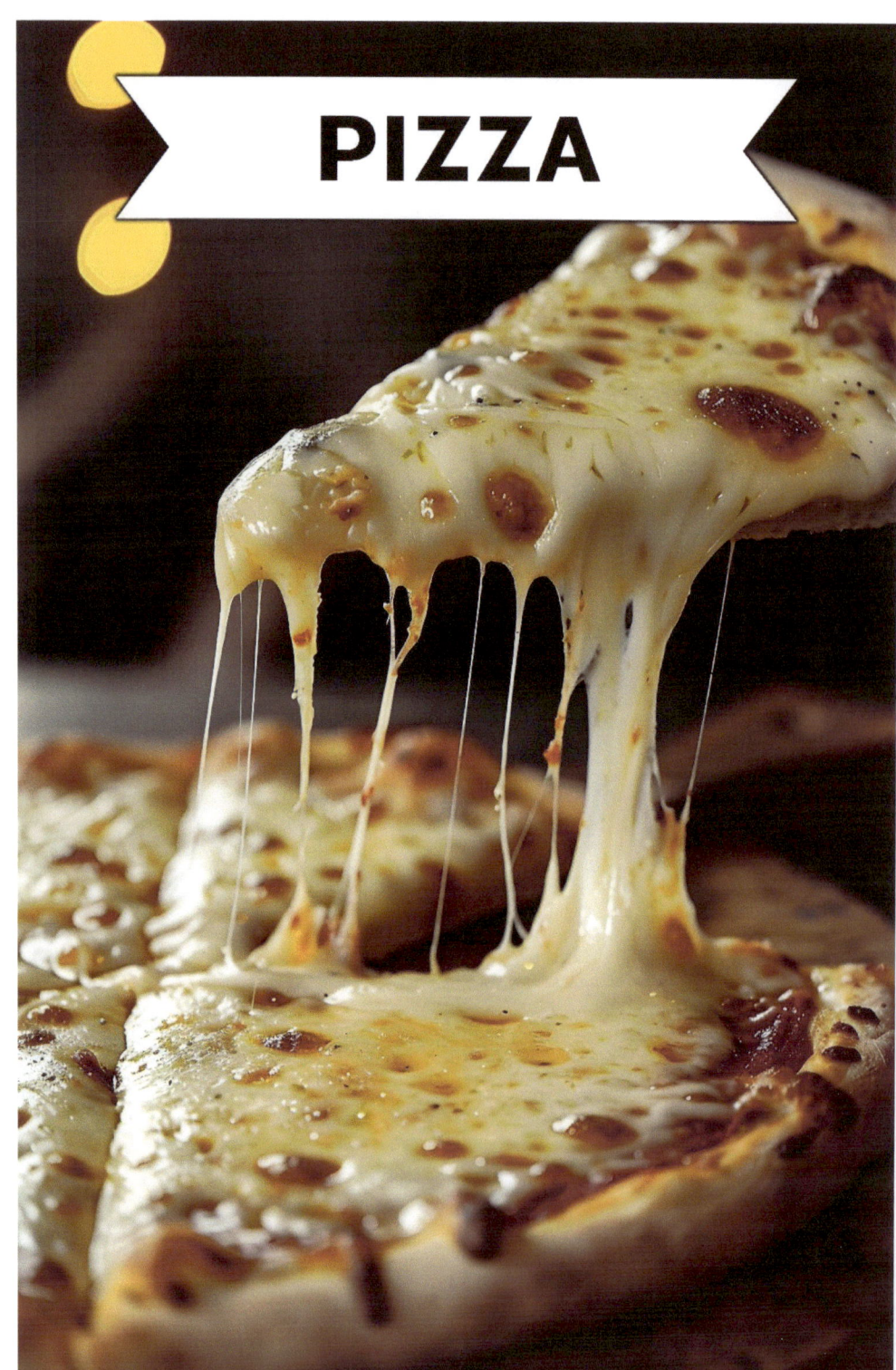

SANDWICH

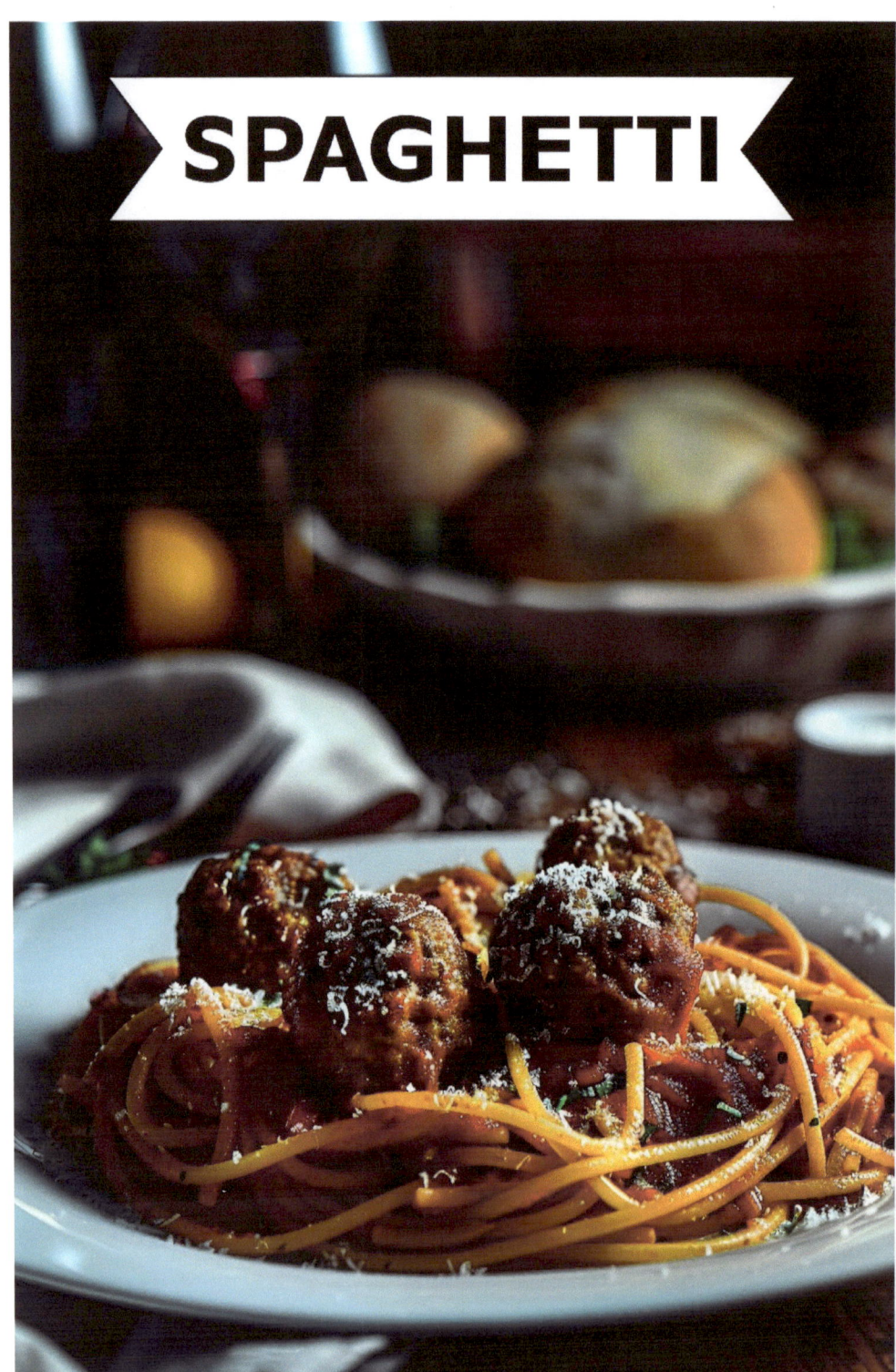

SCRAMBLED EGGS

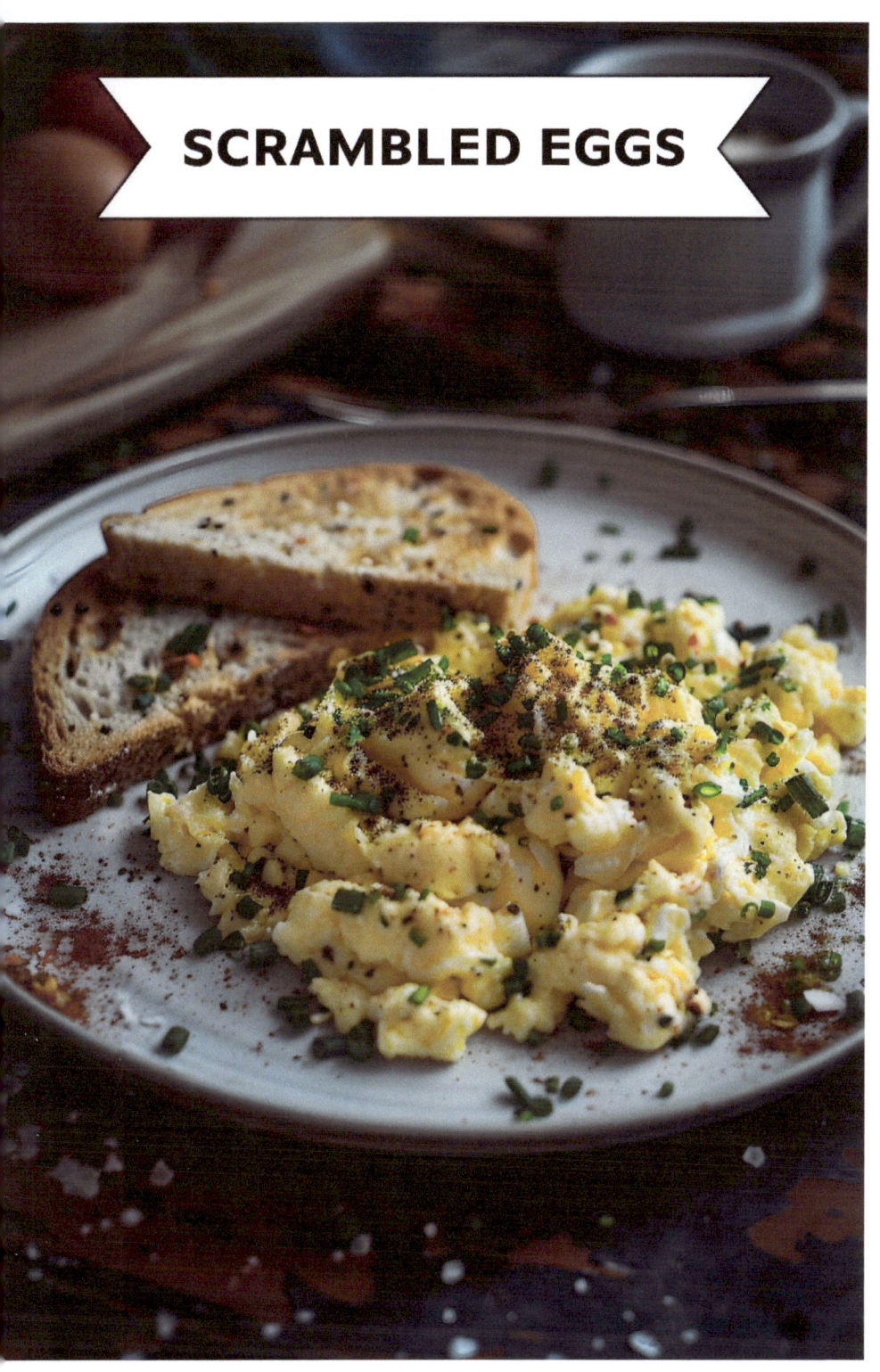

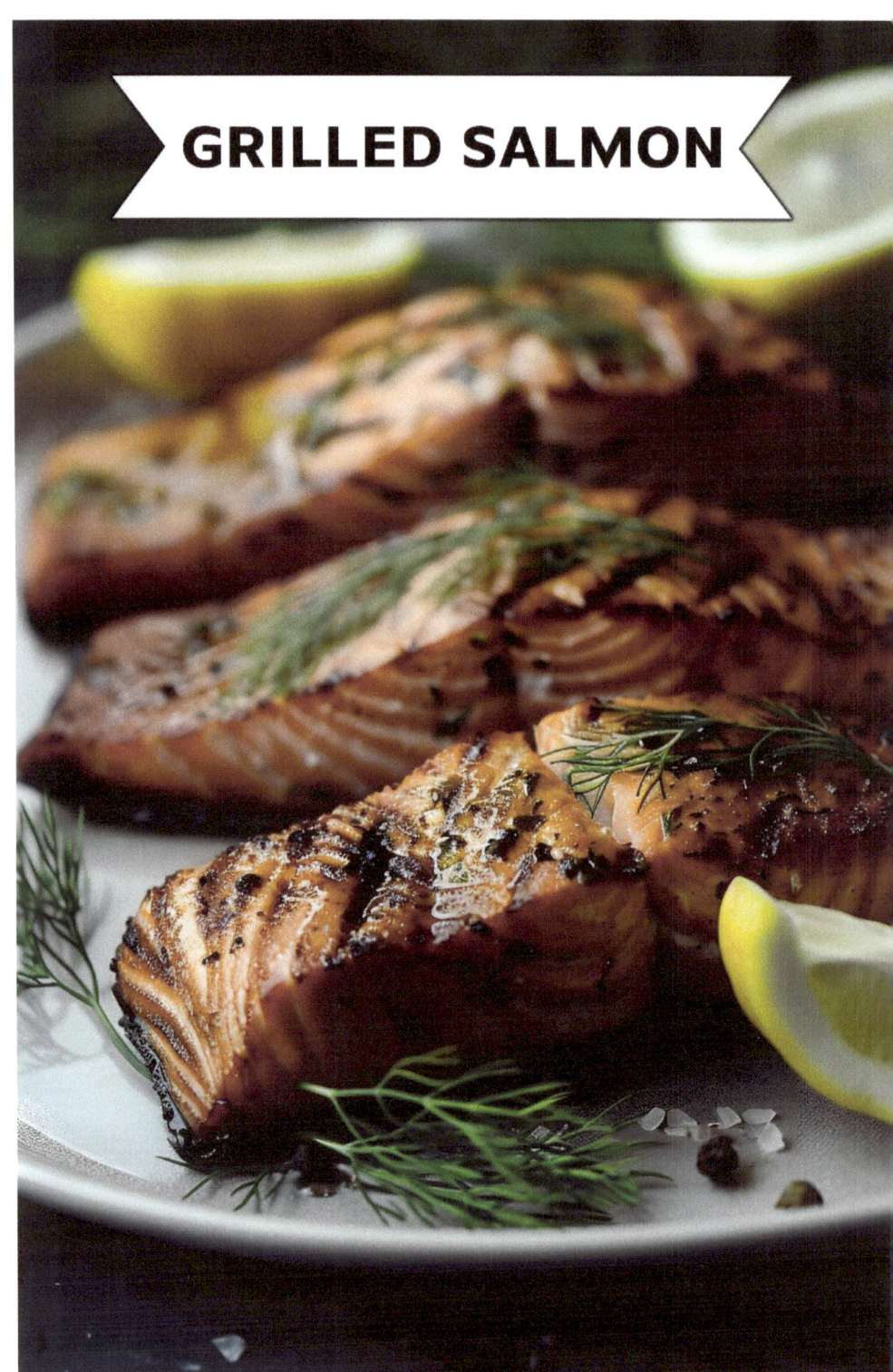

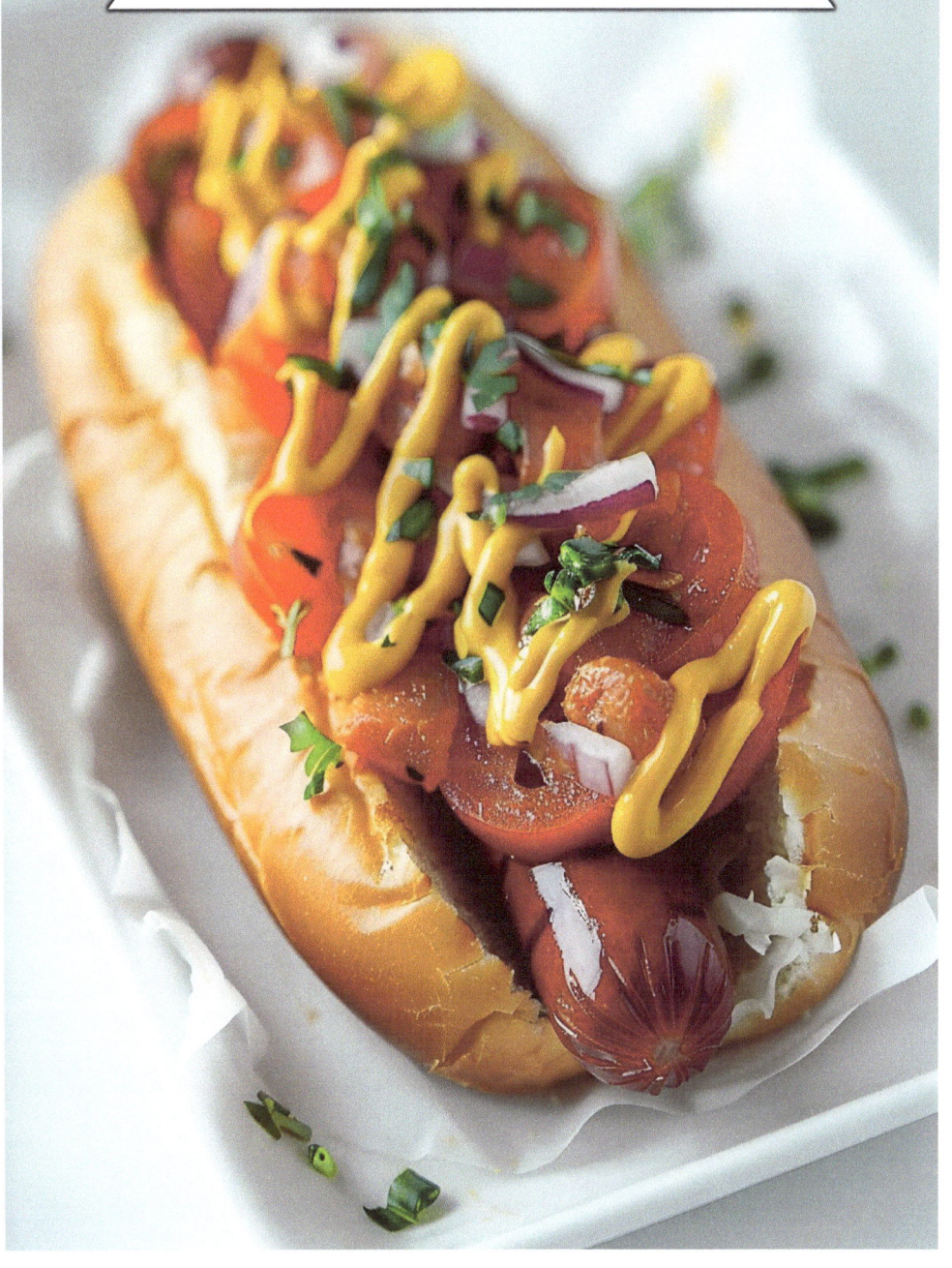

RICE

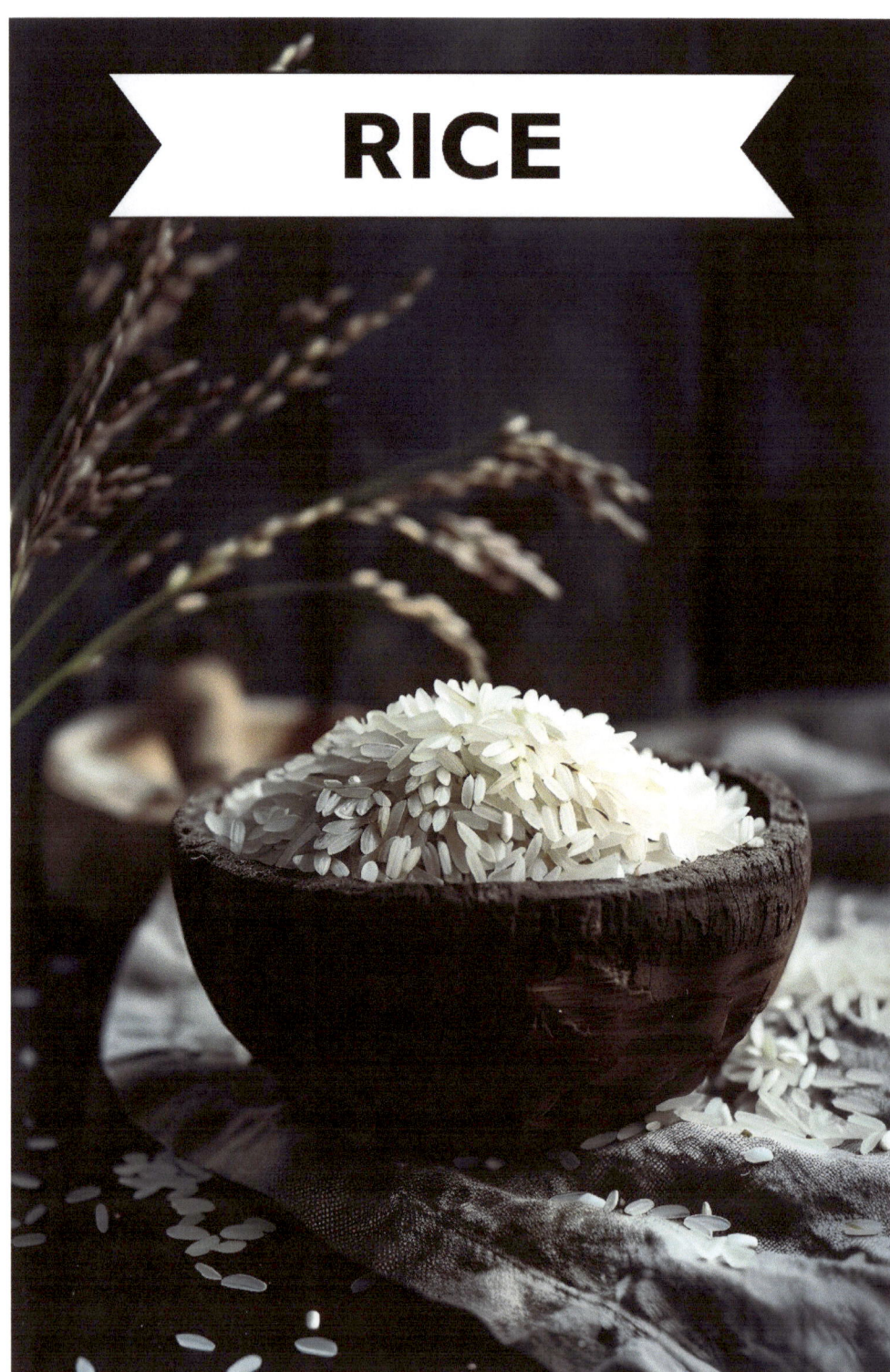

MASHED POTATOES

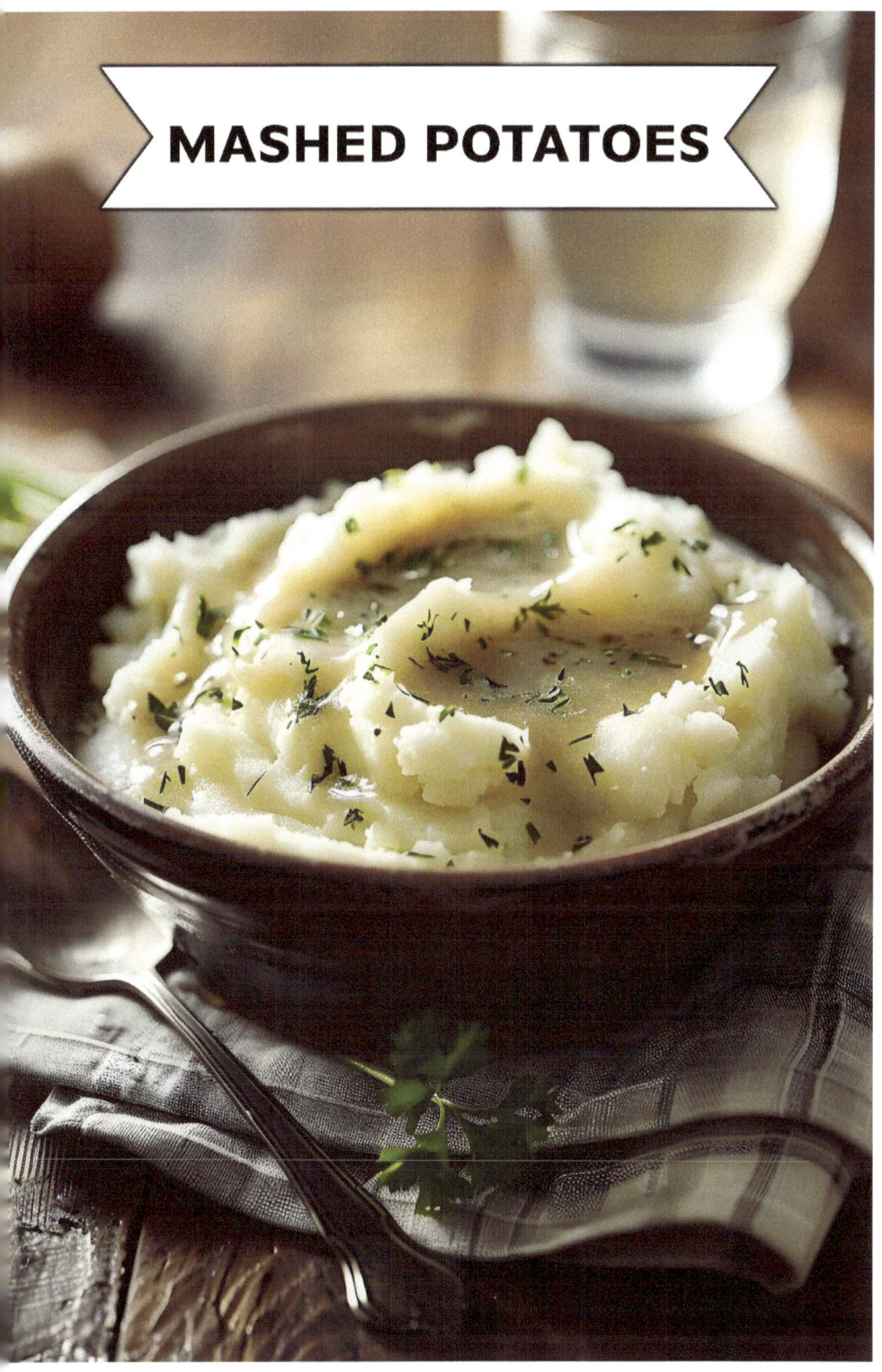

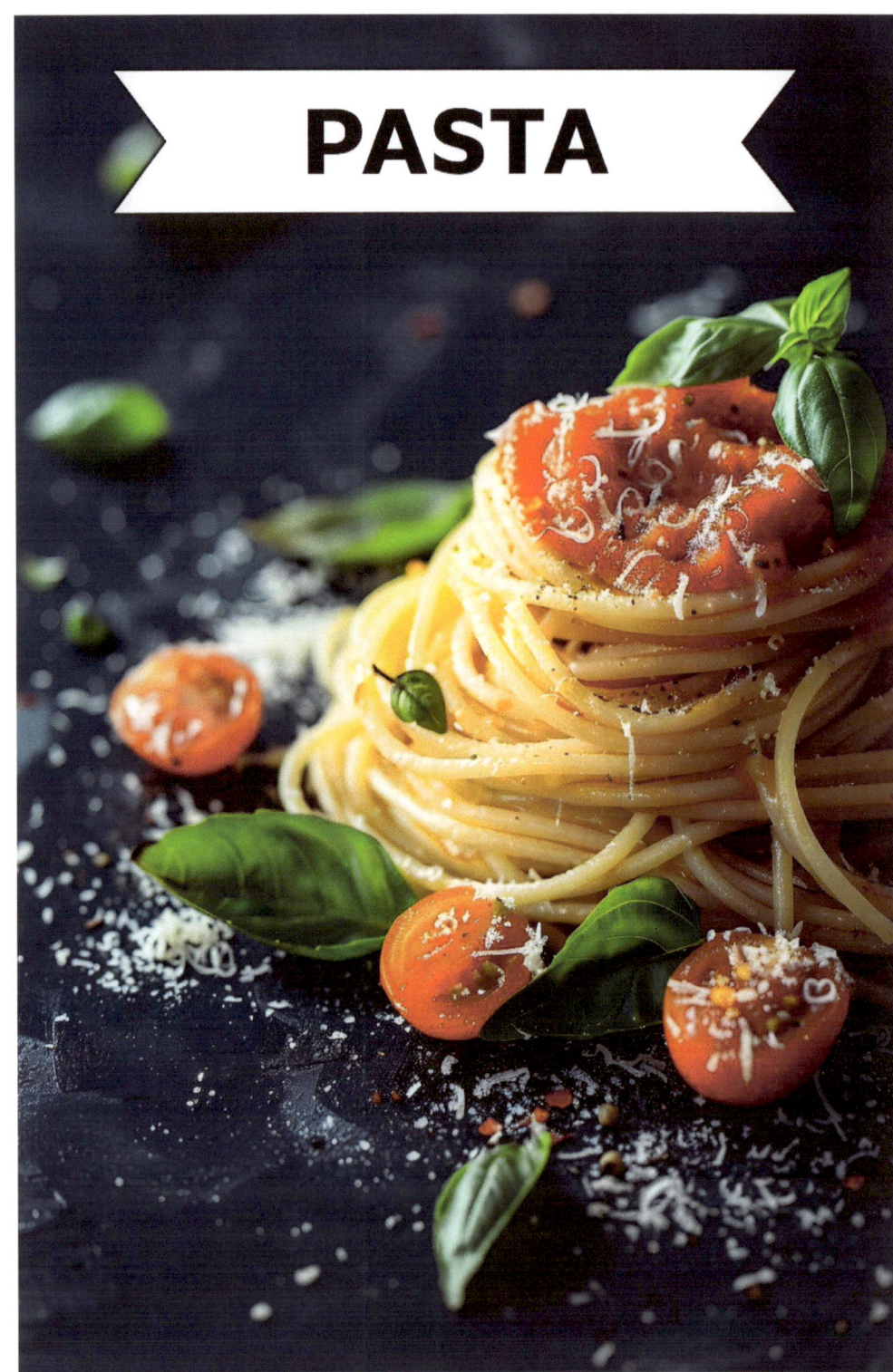

BREAD

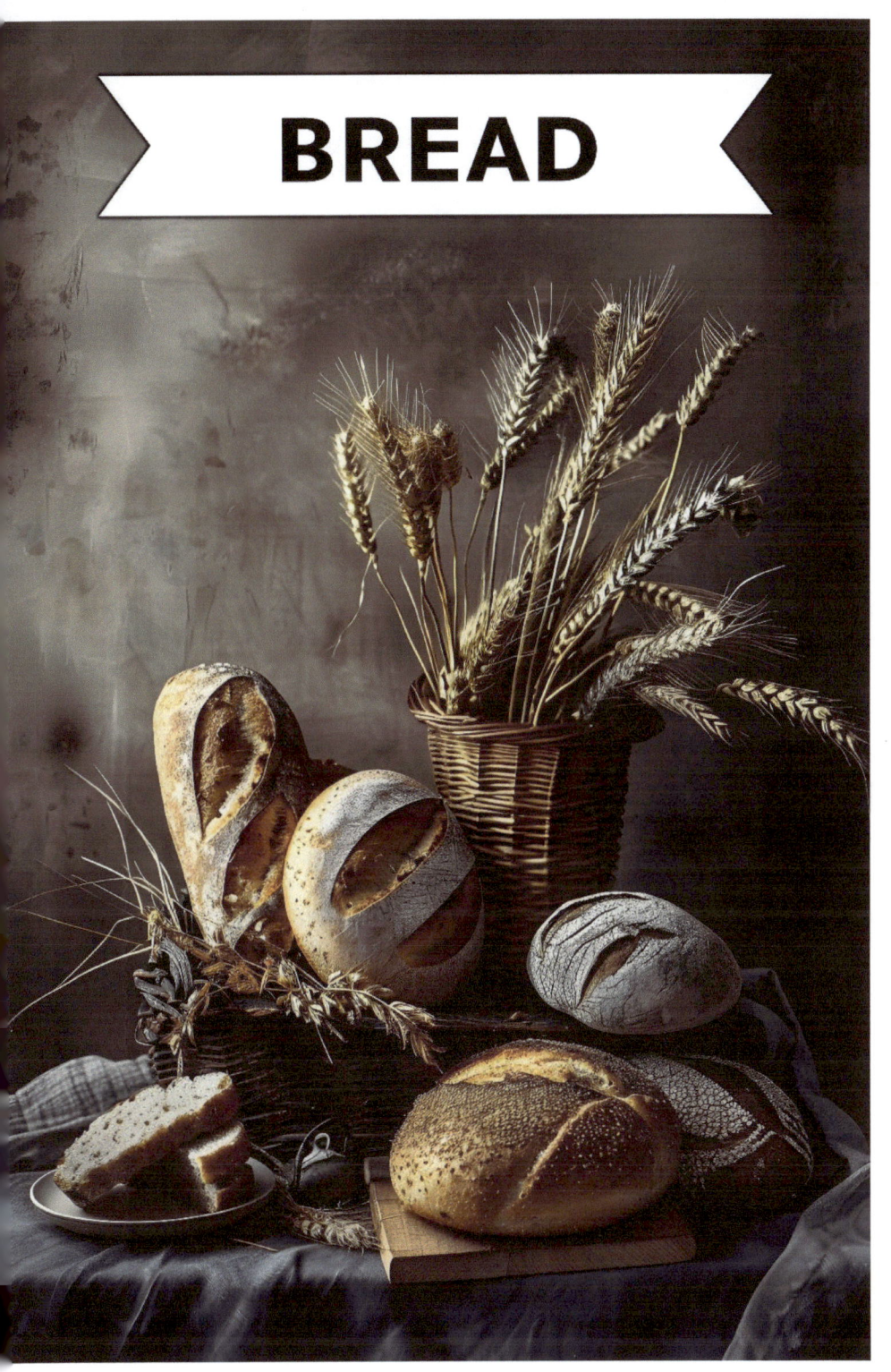

CHEESE

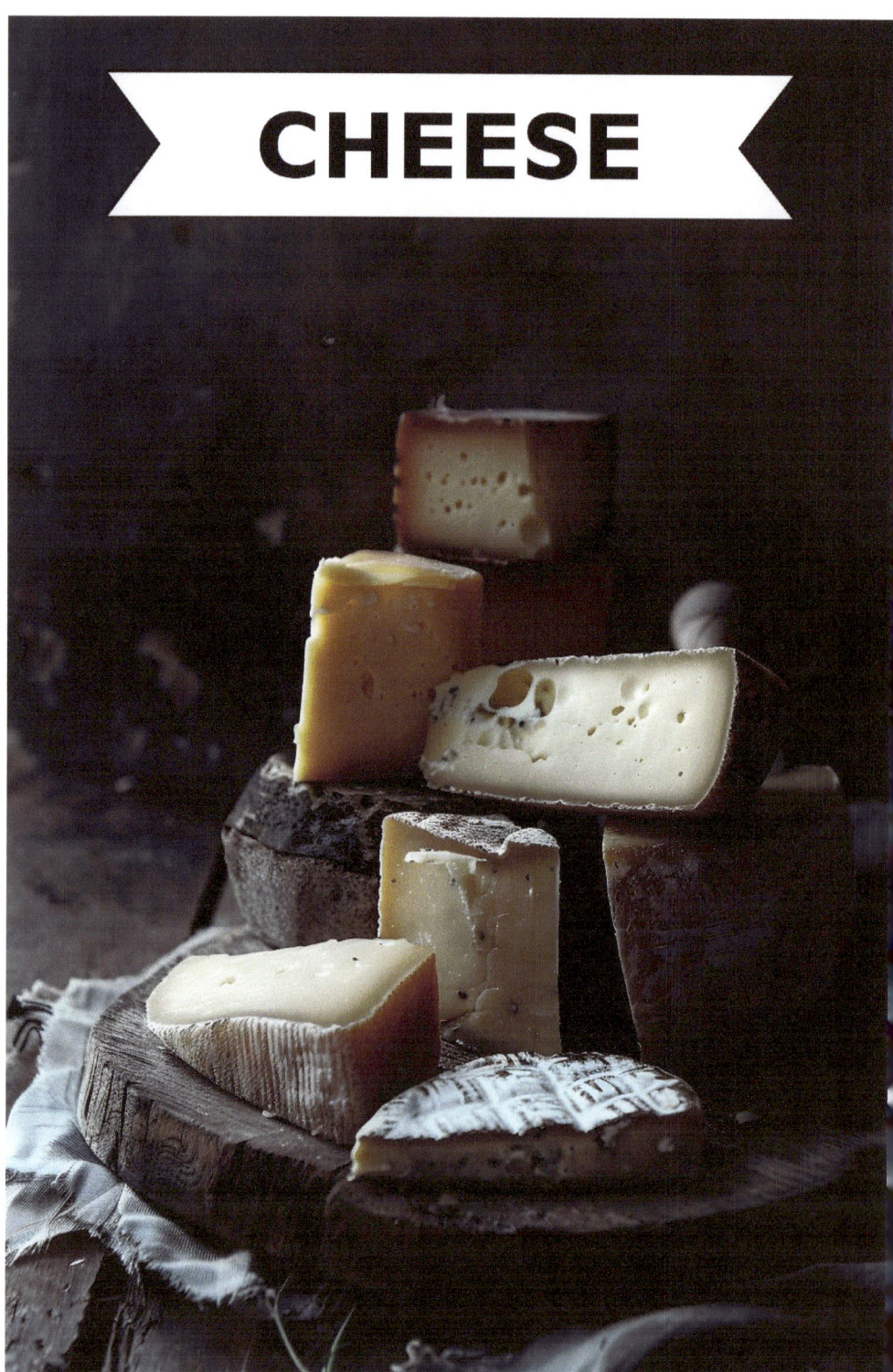

EGG

NUTS

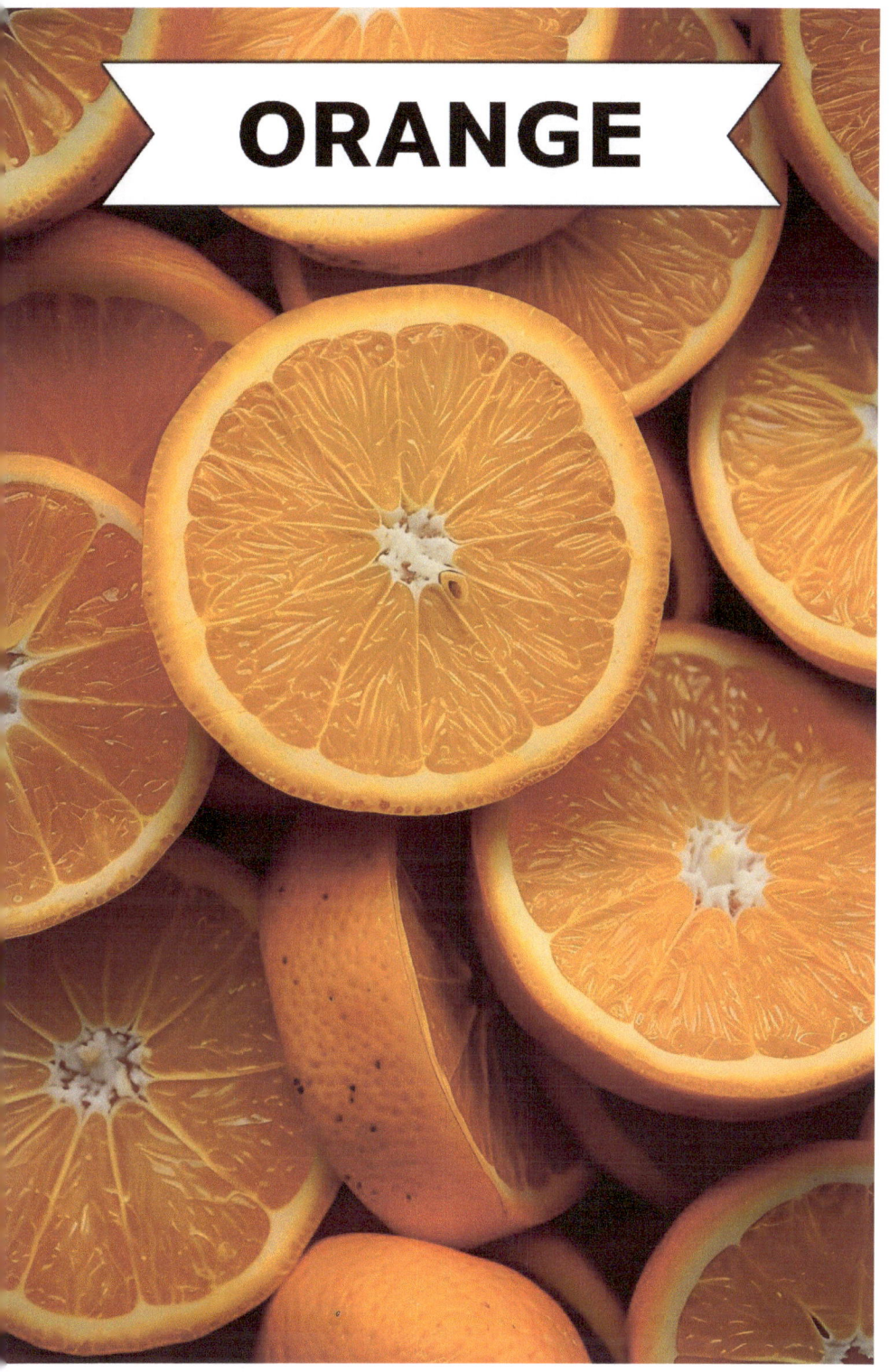

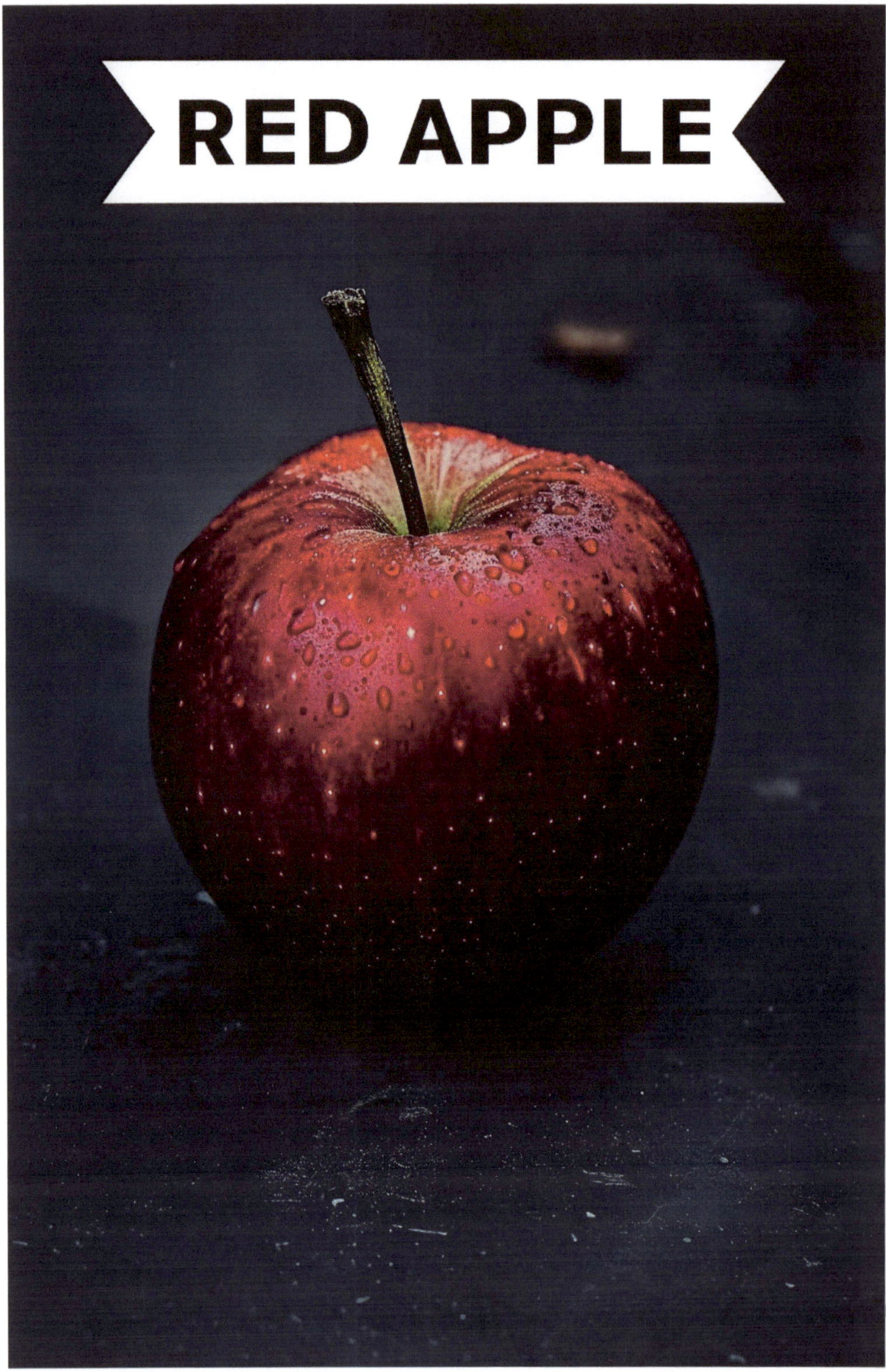

RED APPLE

WATERMELON

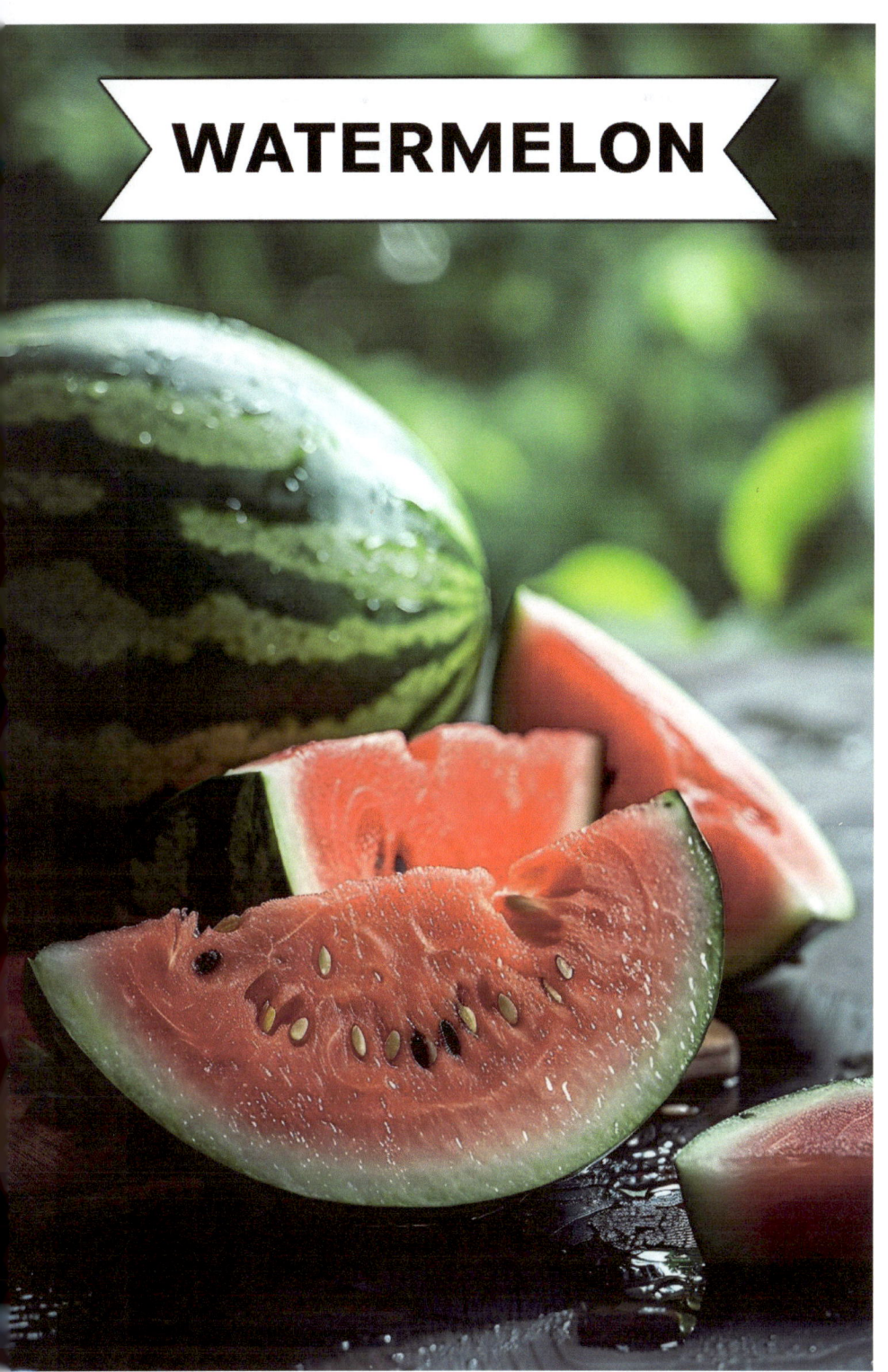

TOMATO

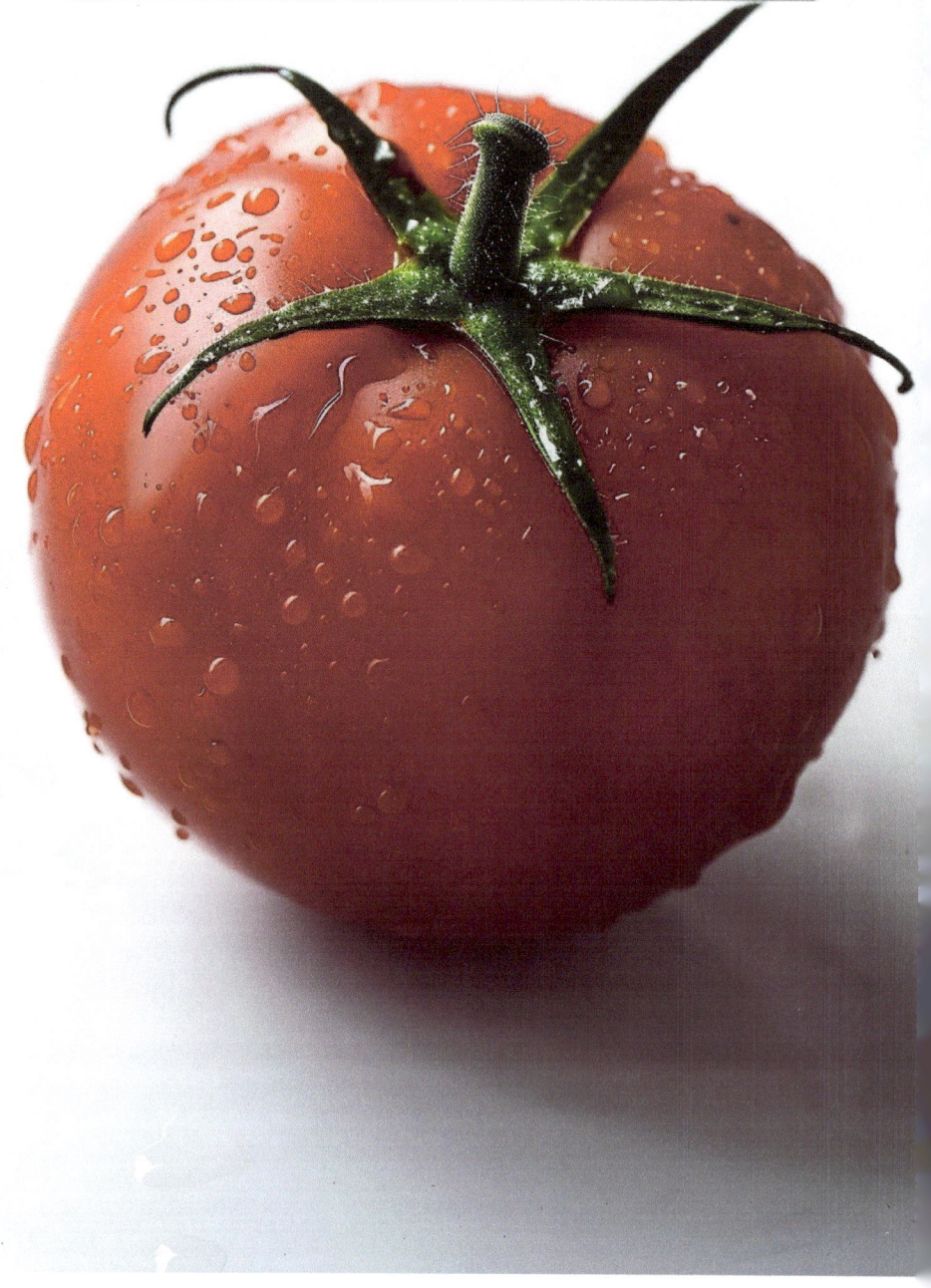

MUSHROOMS

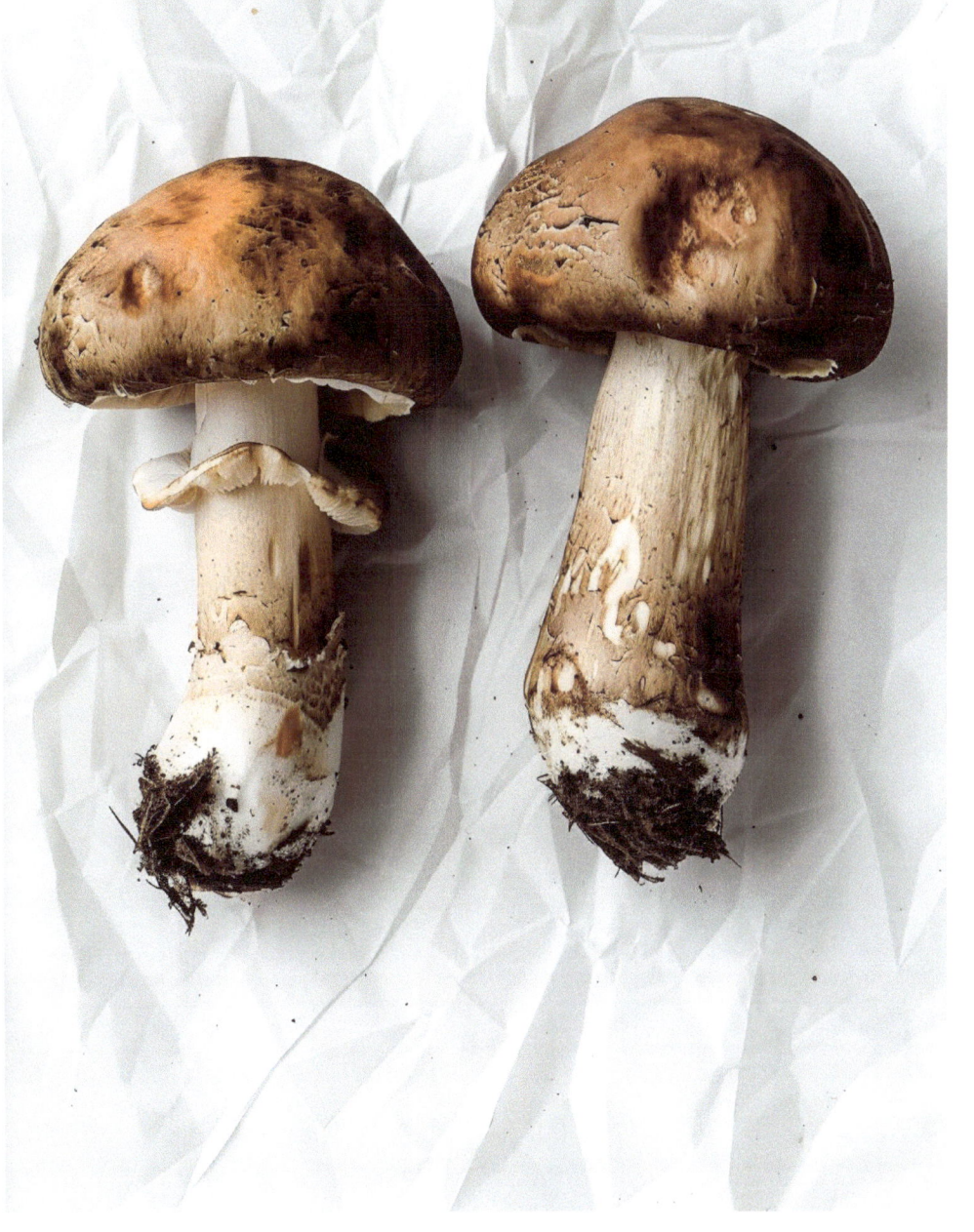

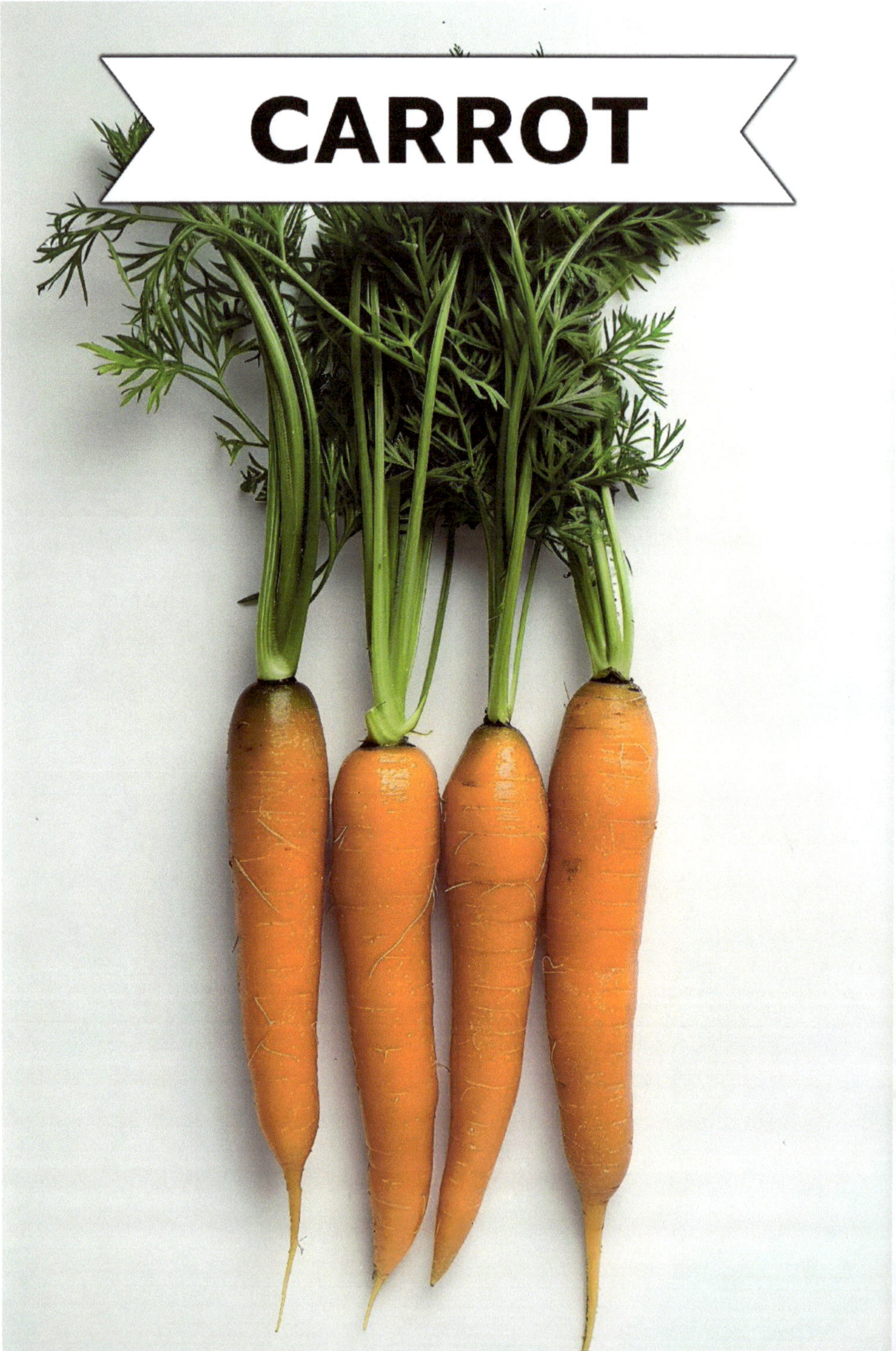

CARROT

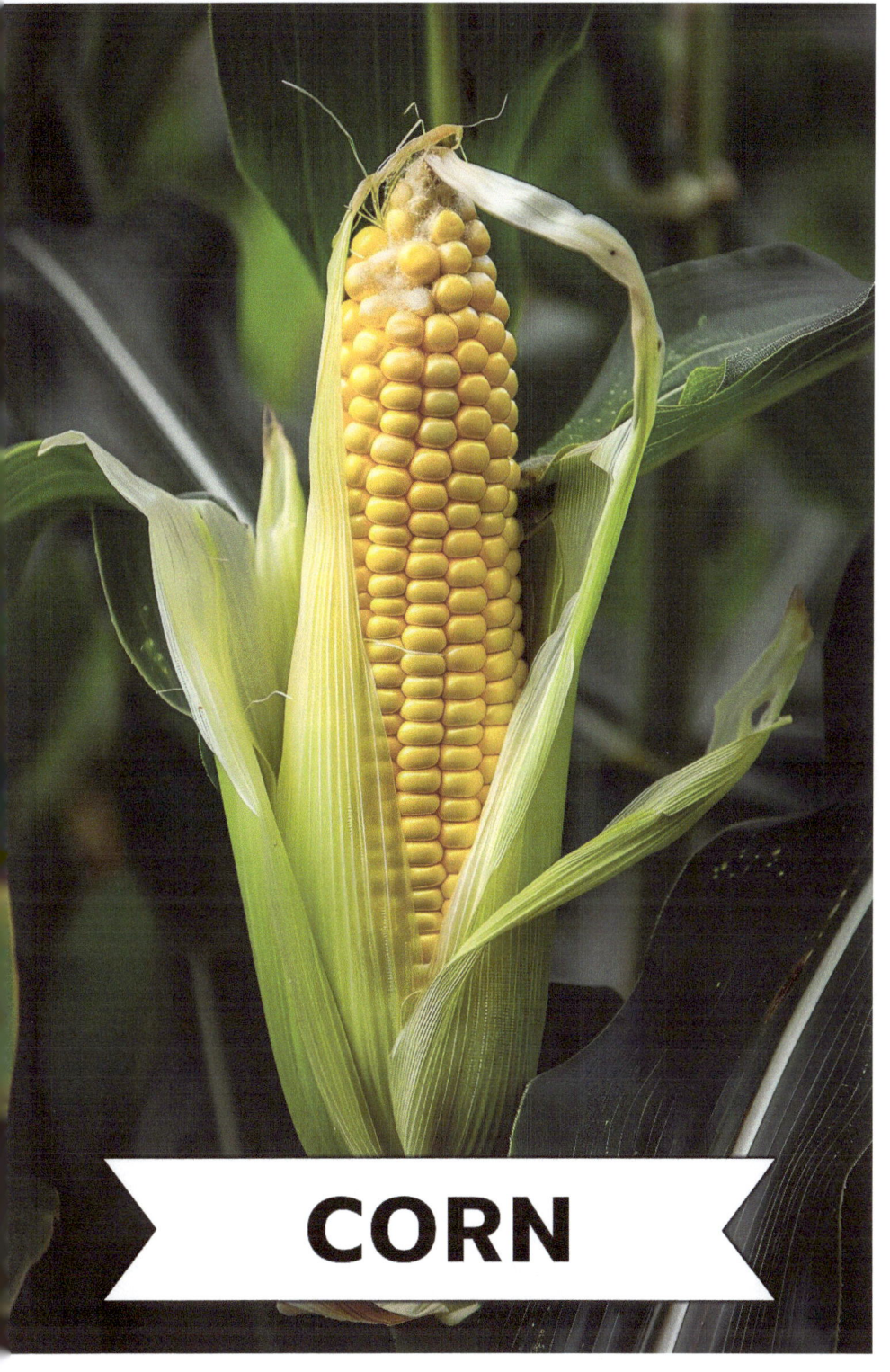

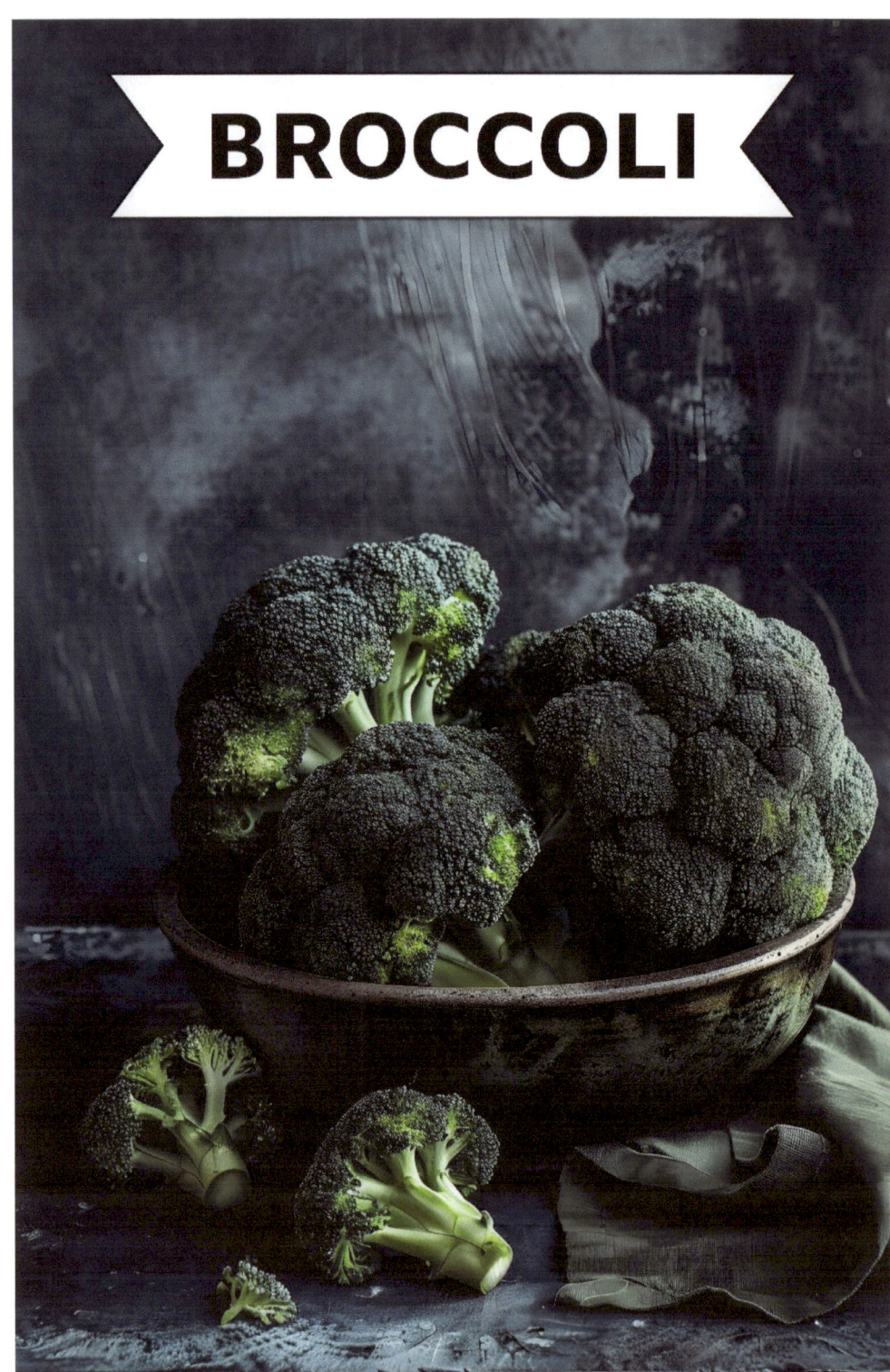

BELL PEPPER

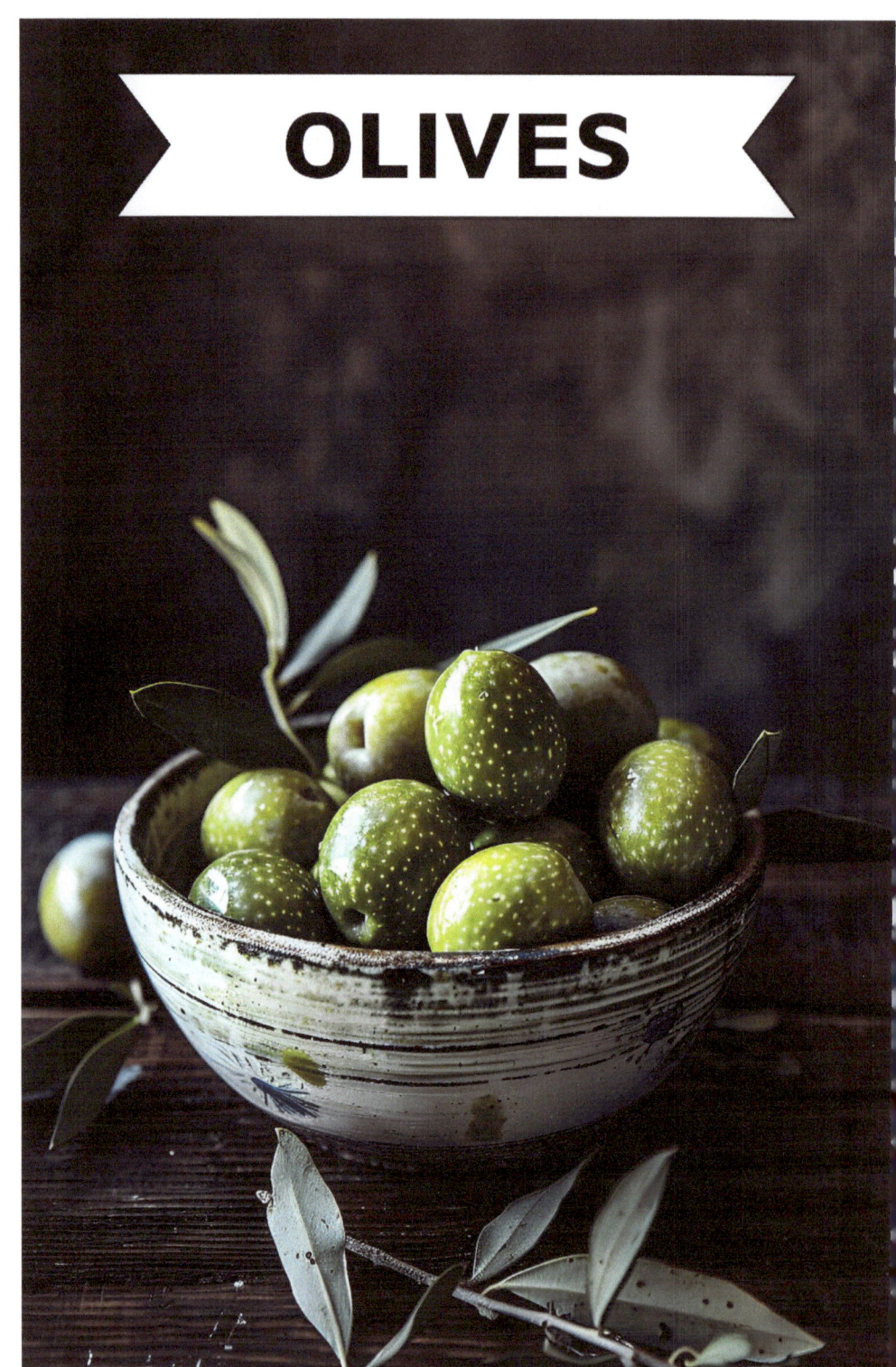

OLIVES

STRAWBERRIES

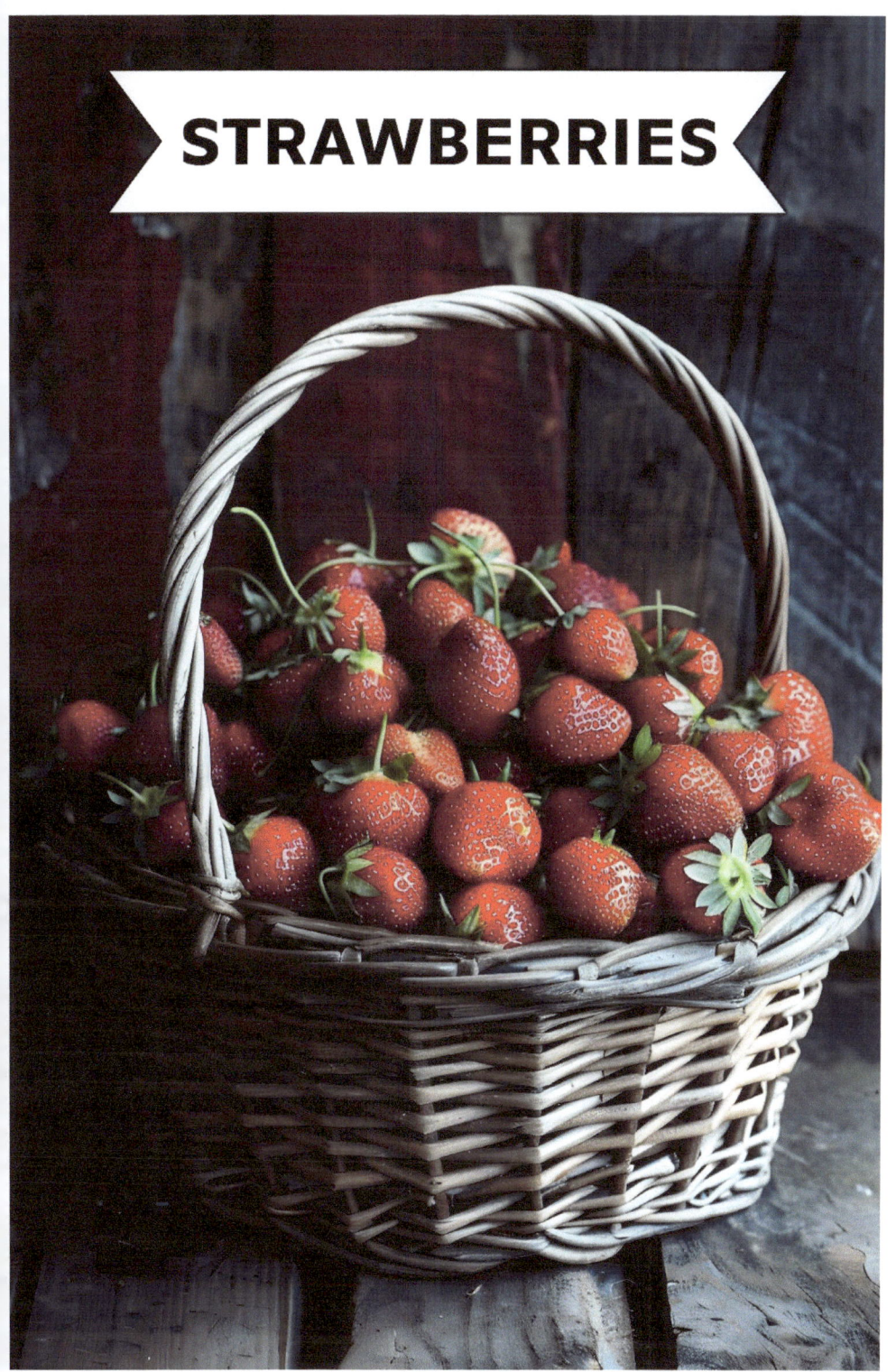

ONION

LEMON

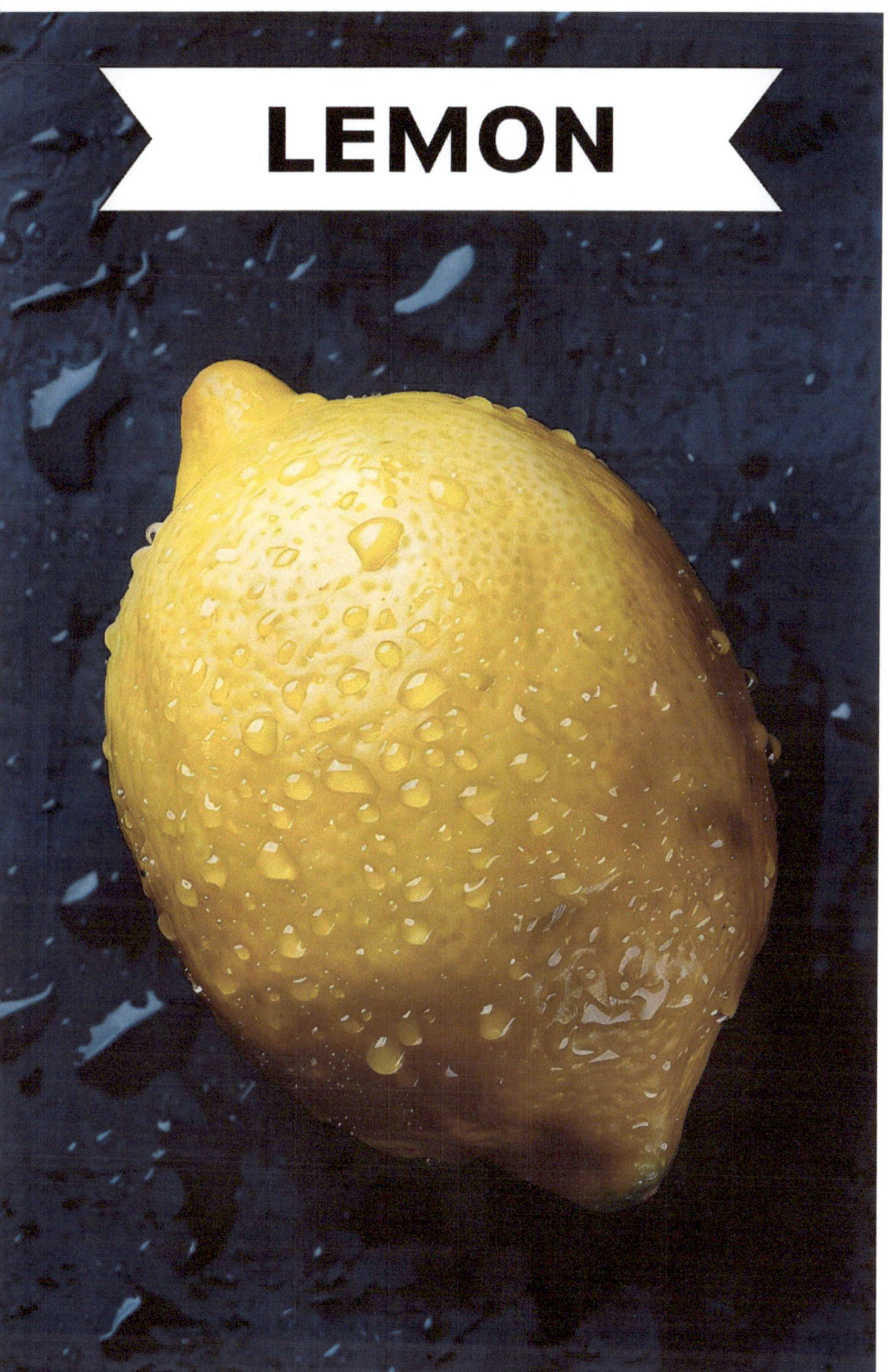

GRAPE

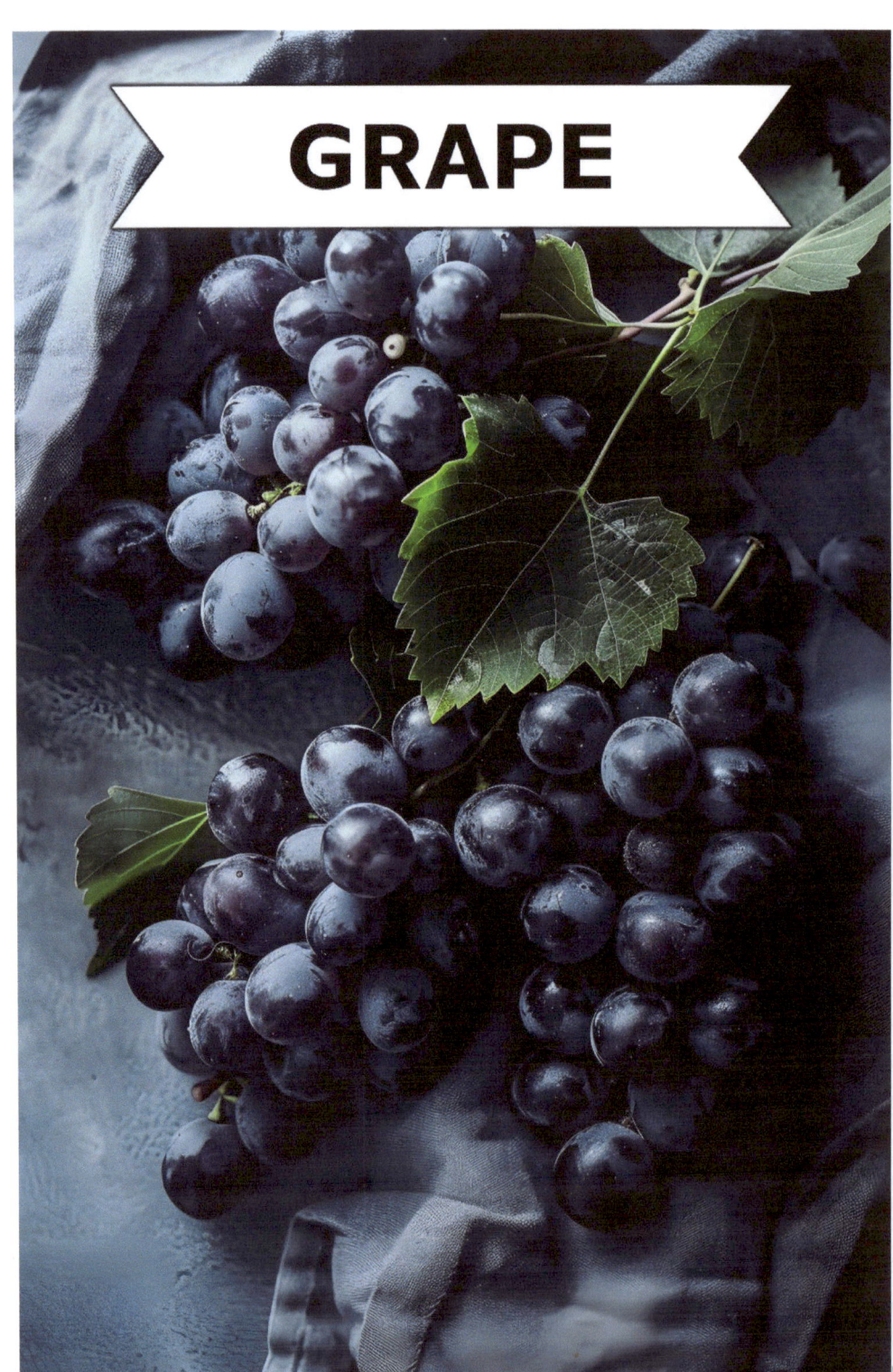

COFFEE

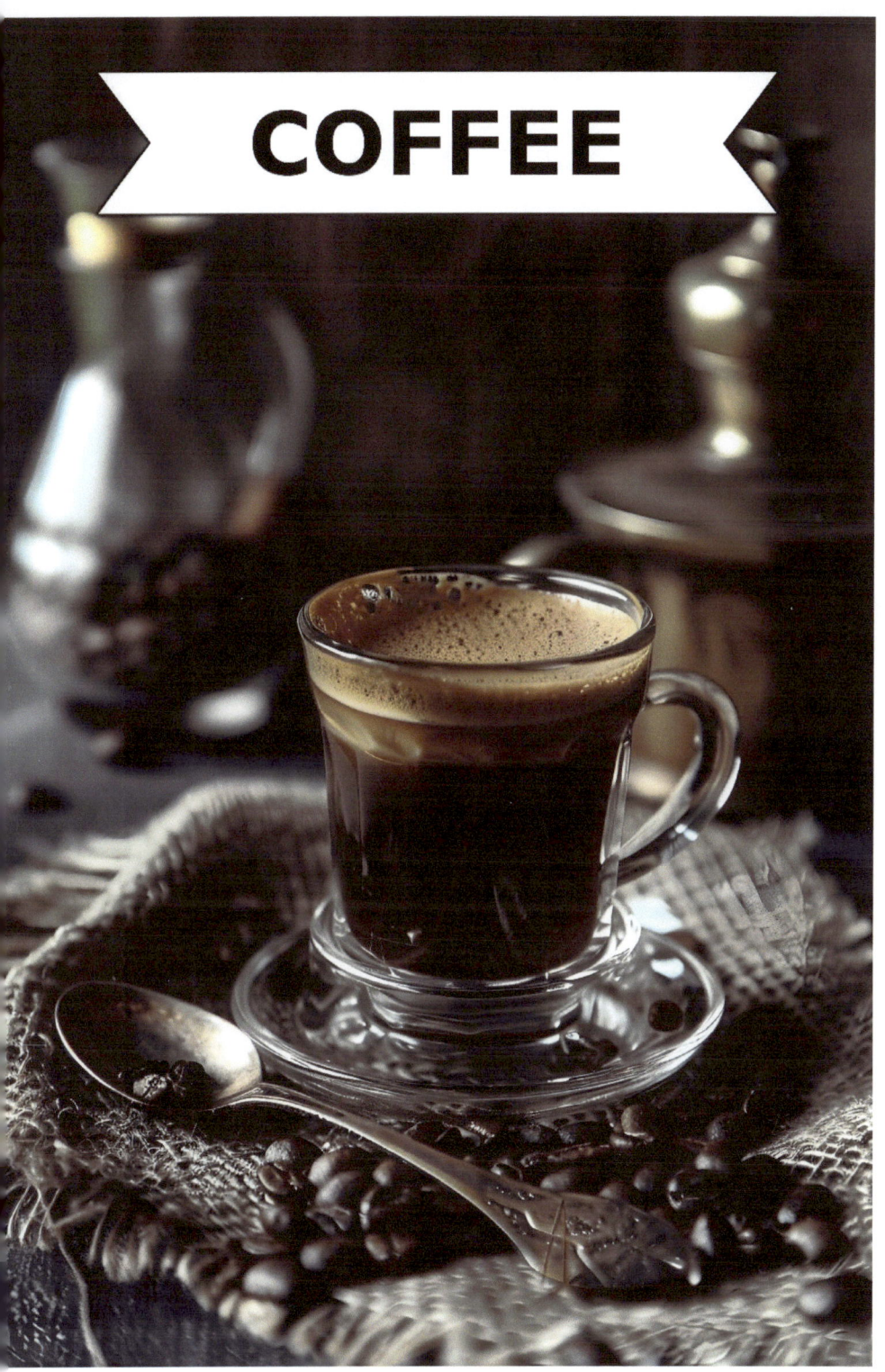

CUPCAKE

COOKIE

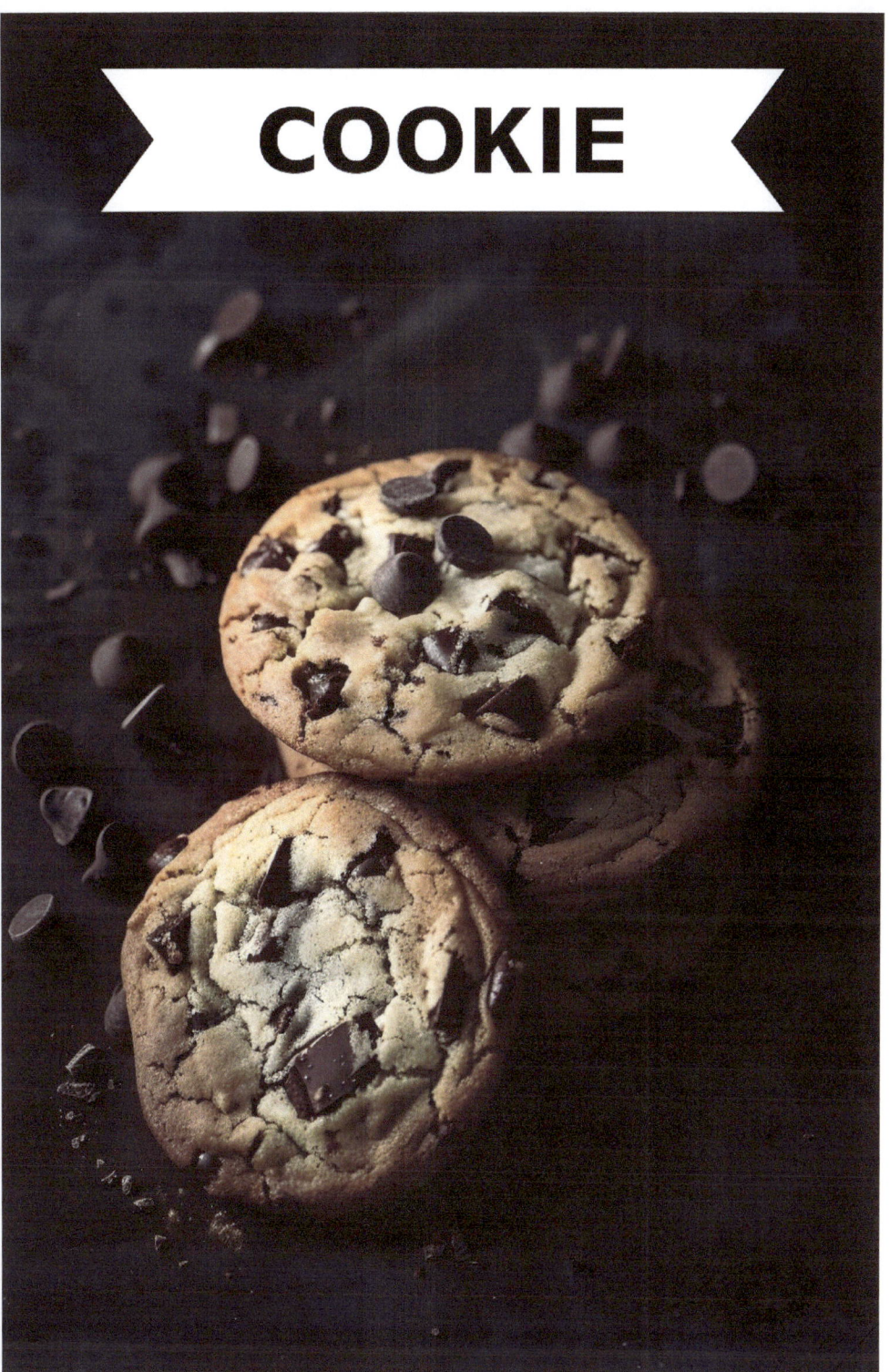

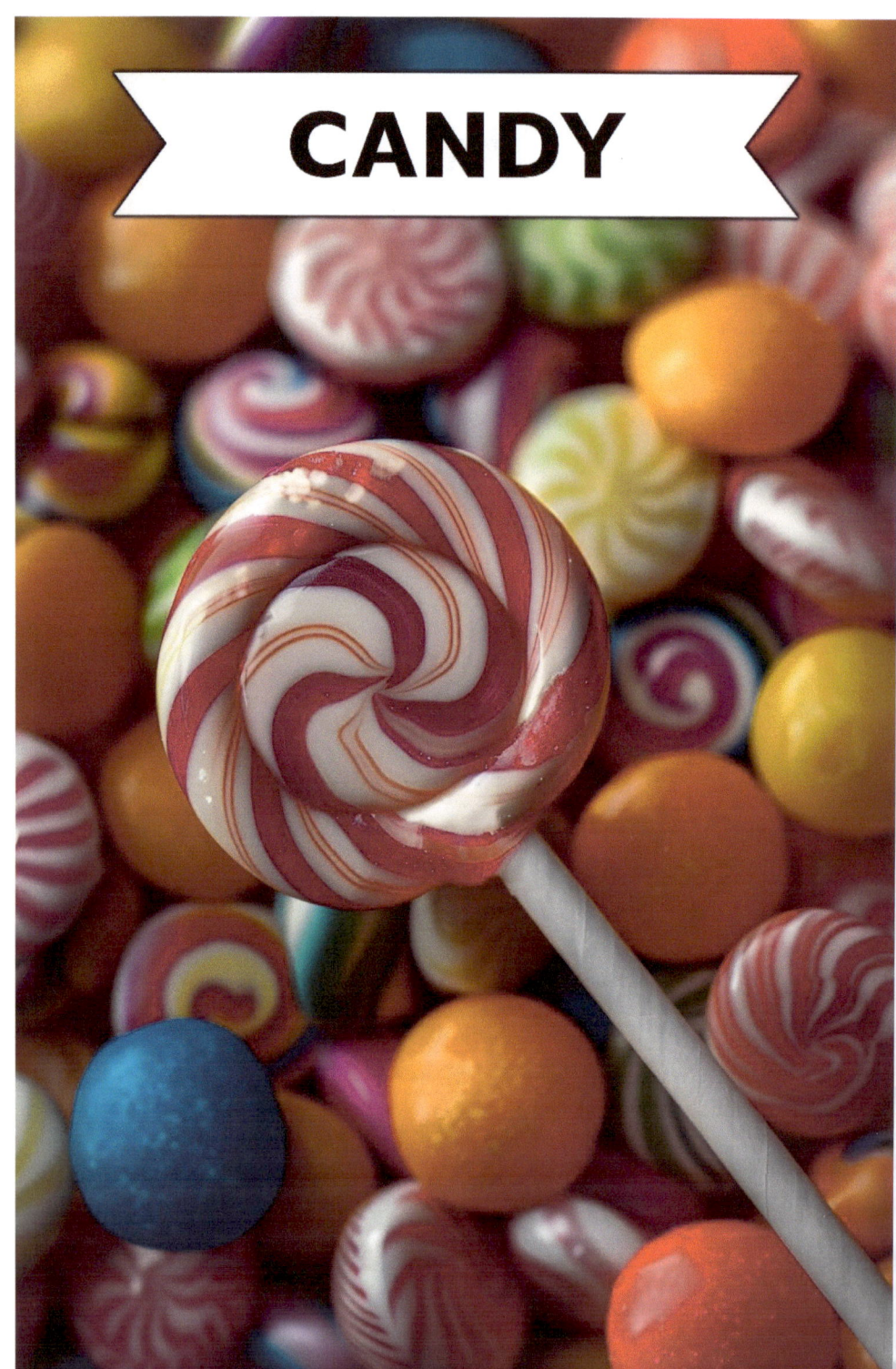

CANDY

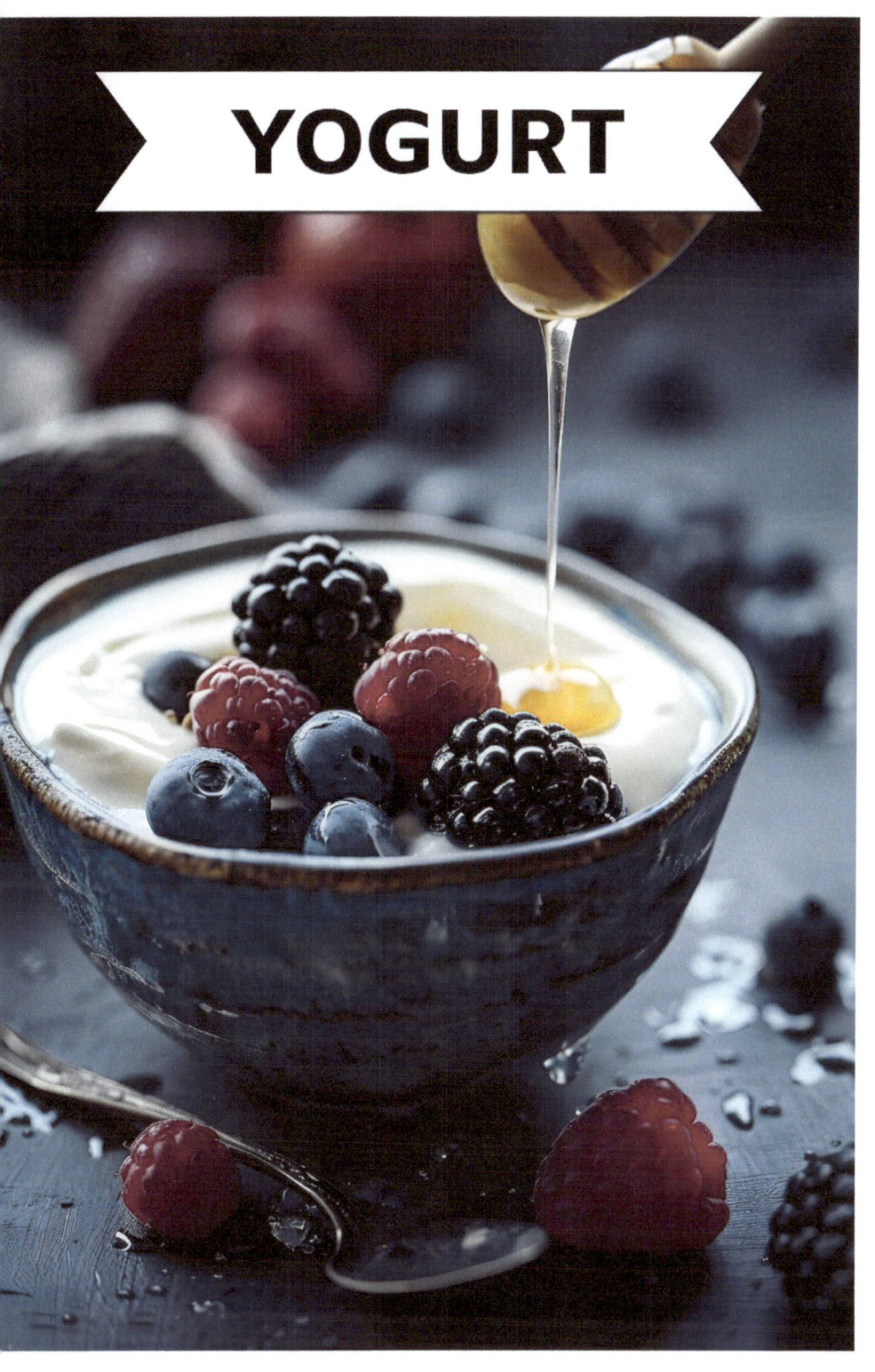

YOGURT

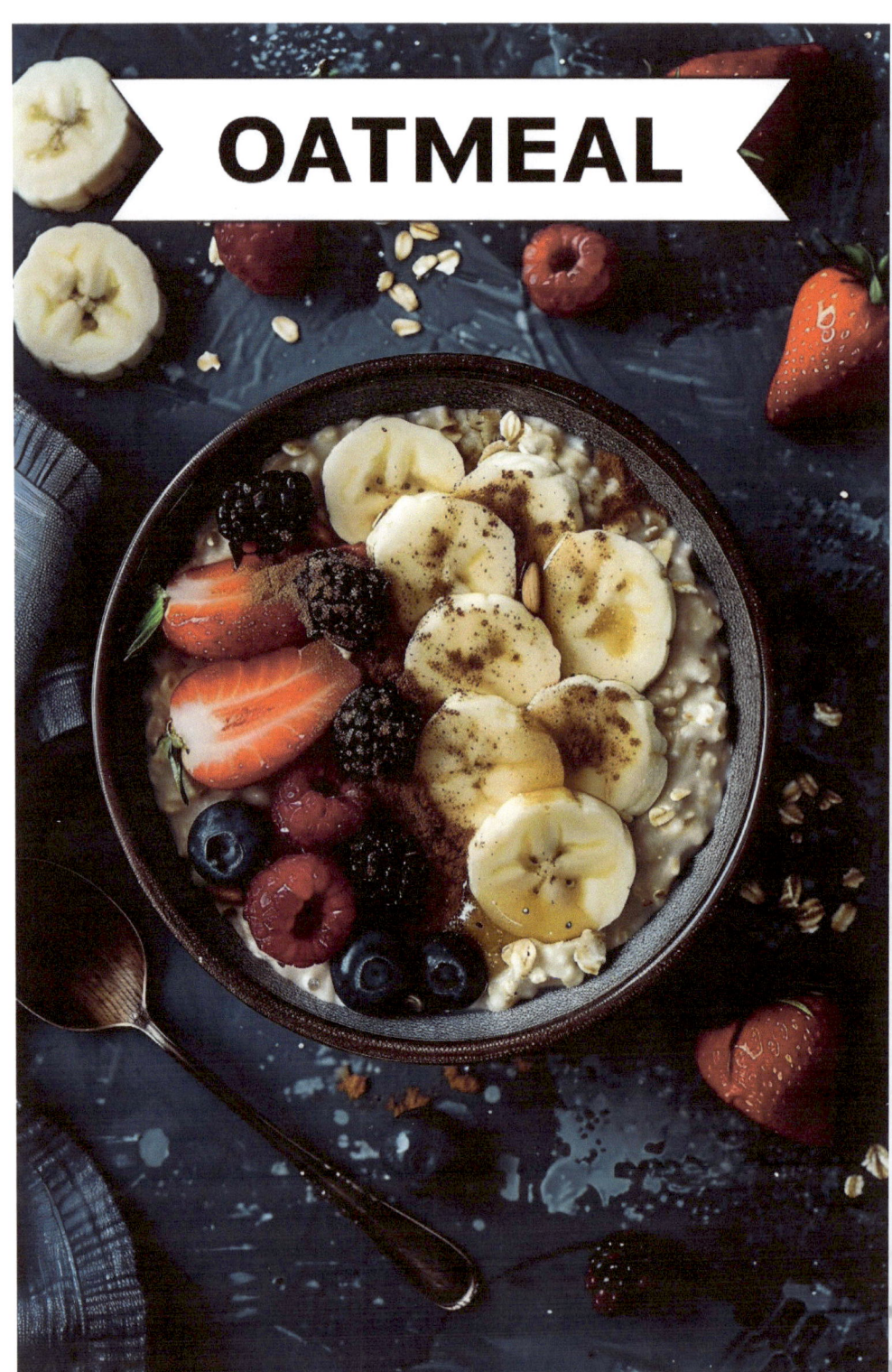

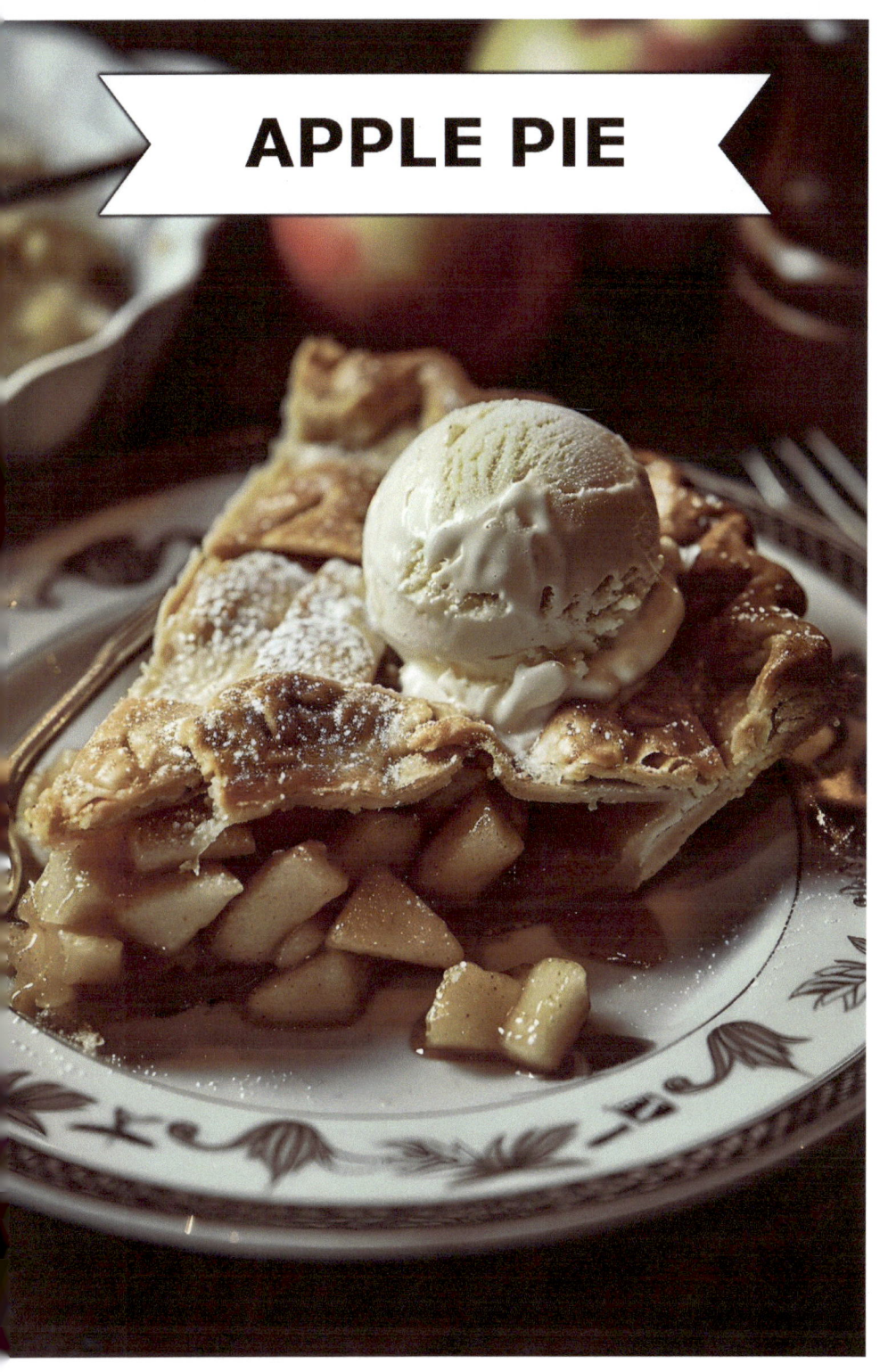

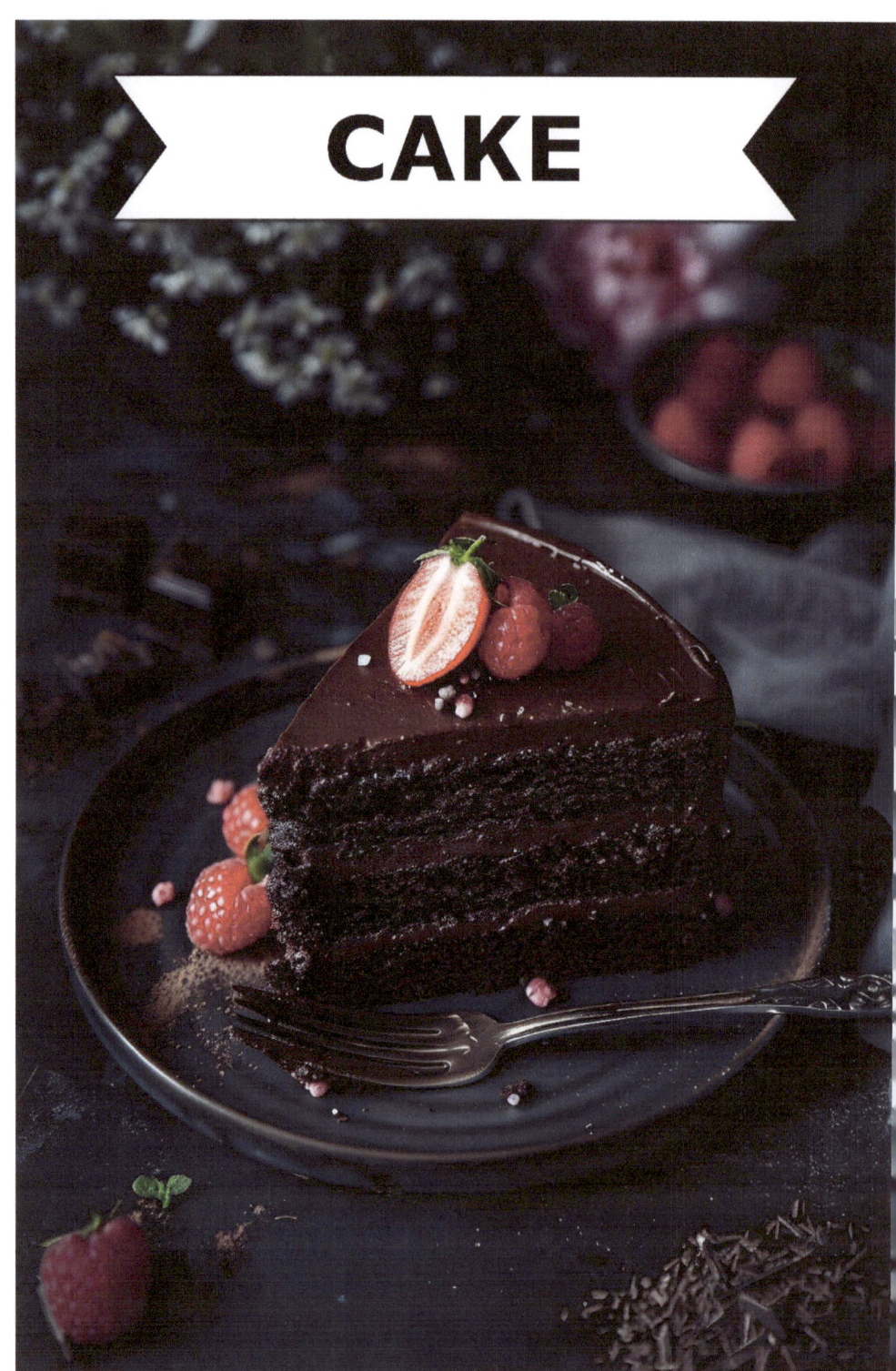

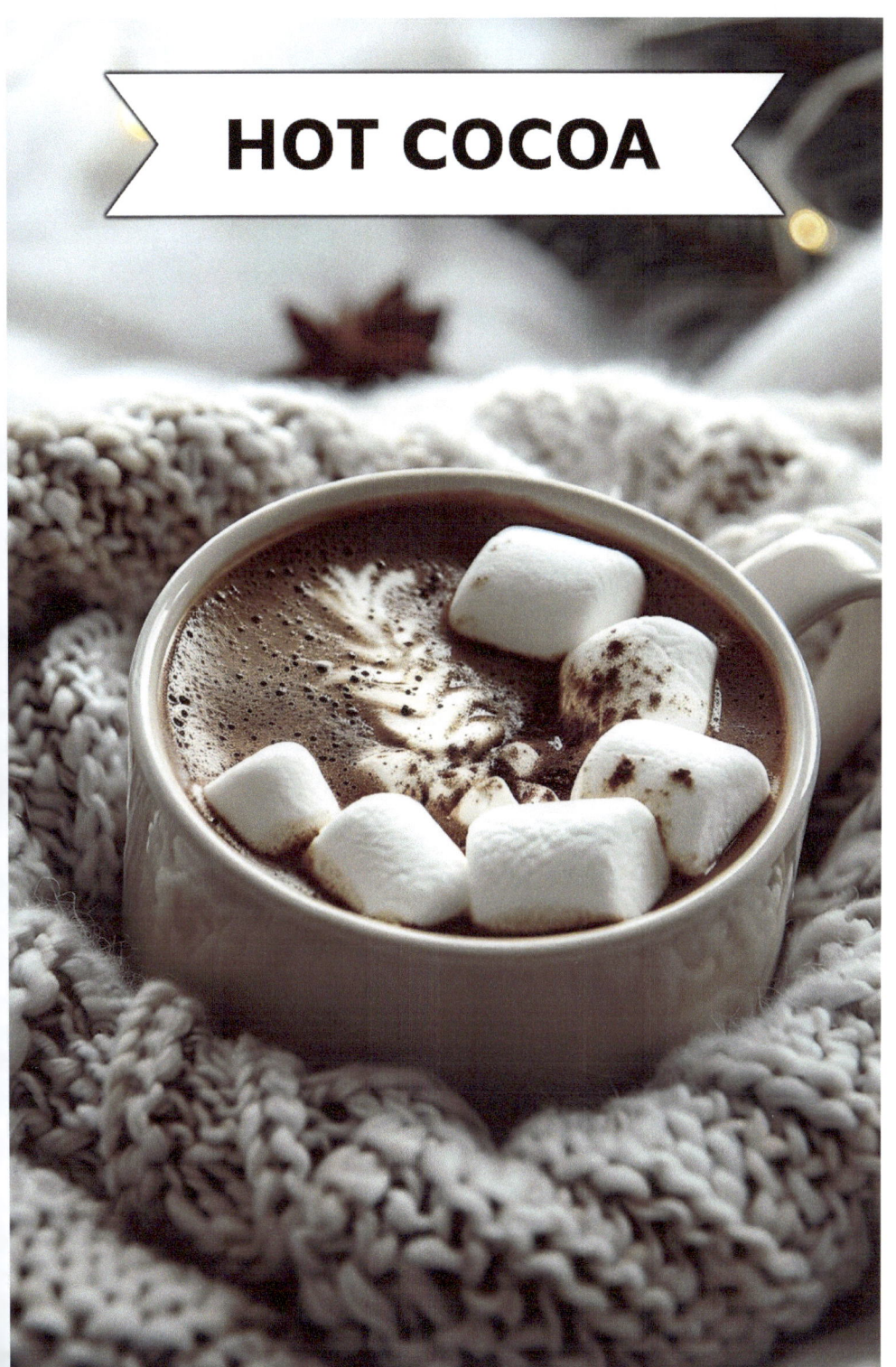
HOT COCOA

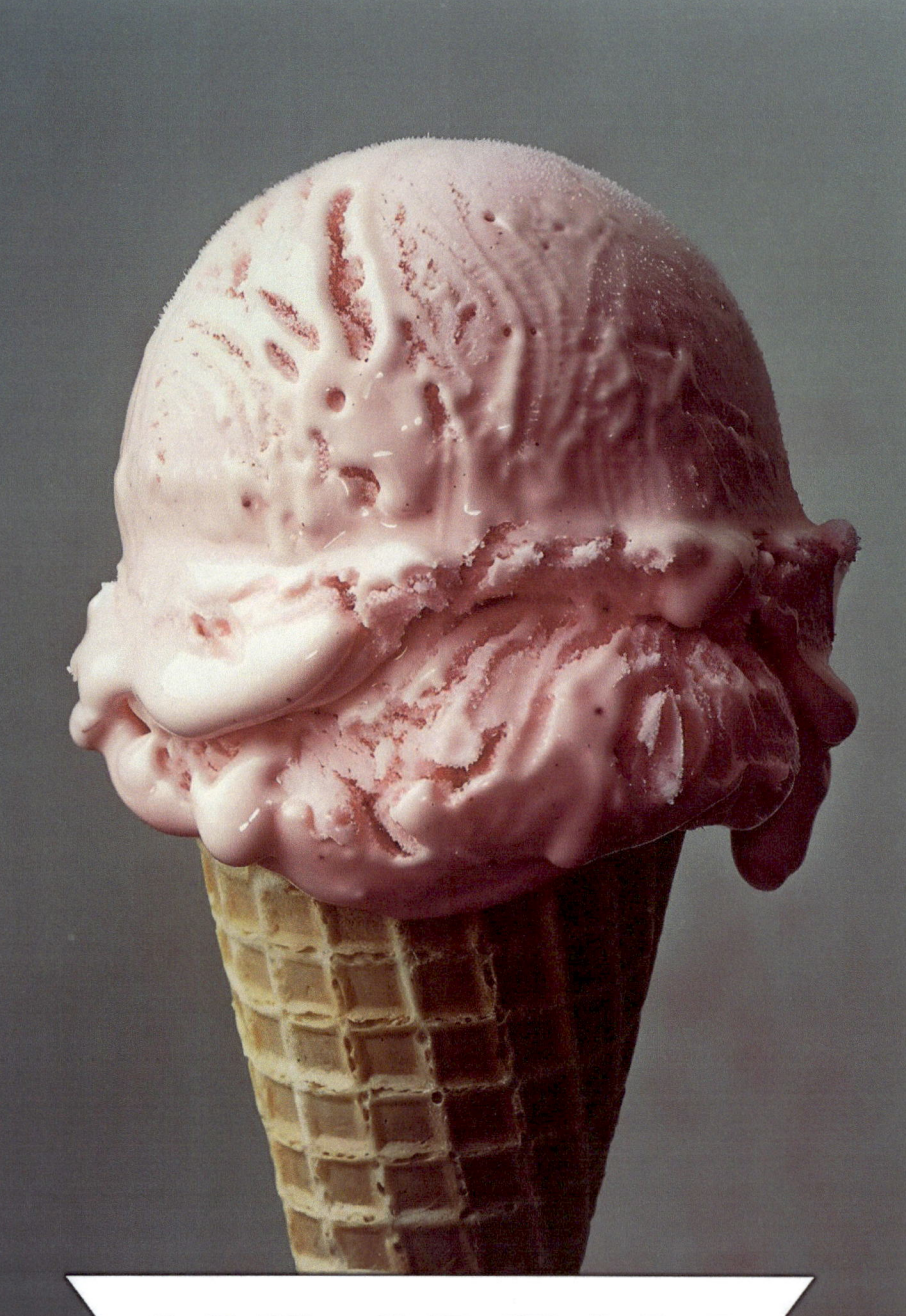

GINGERBREAD

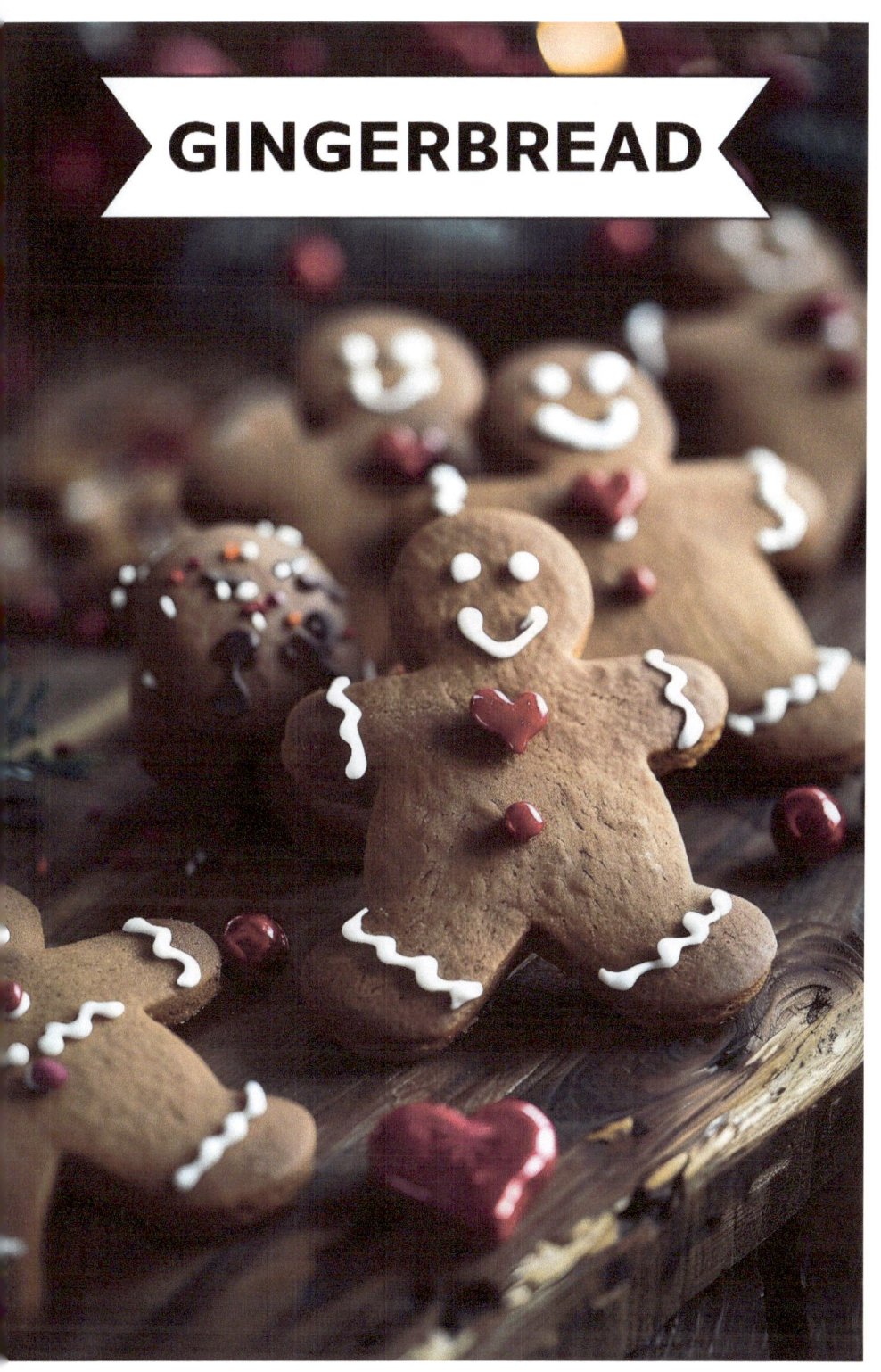

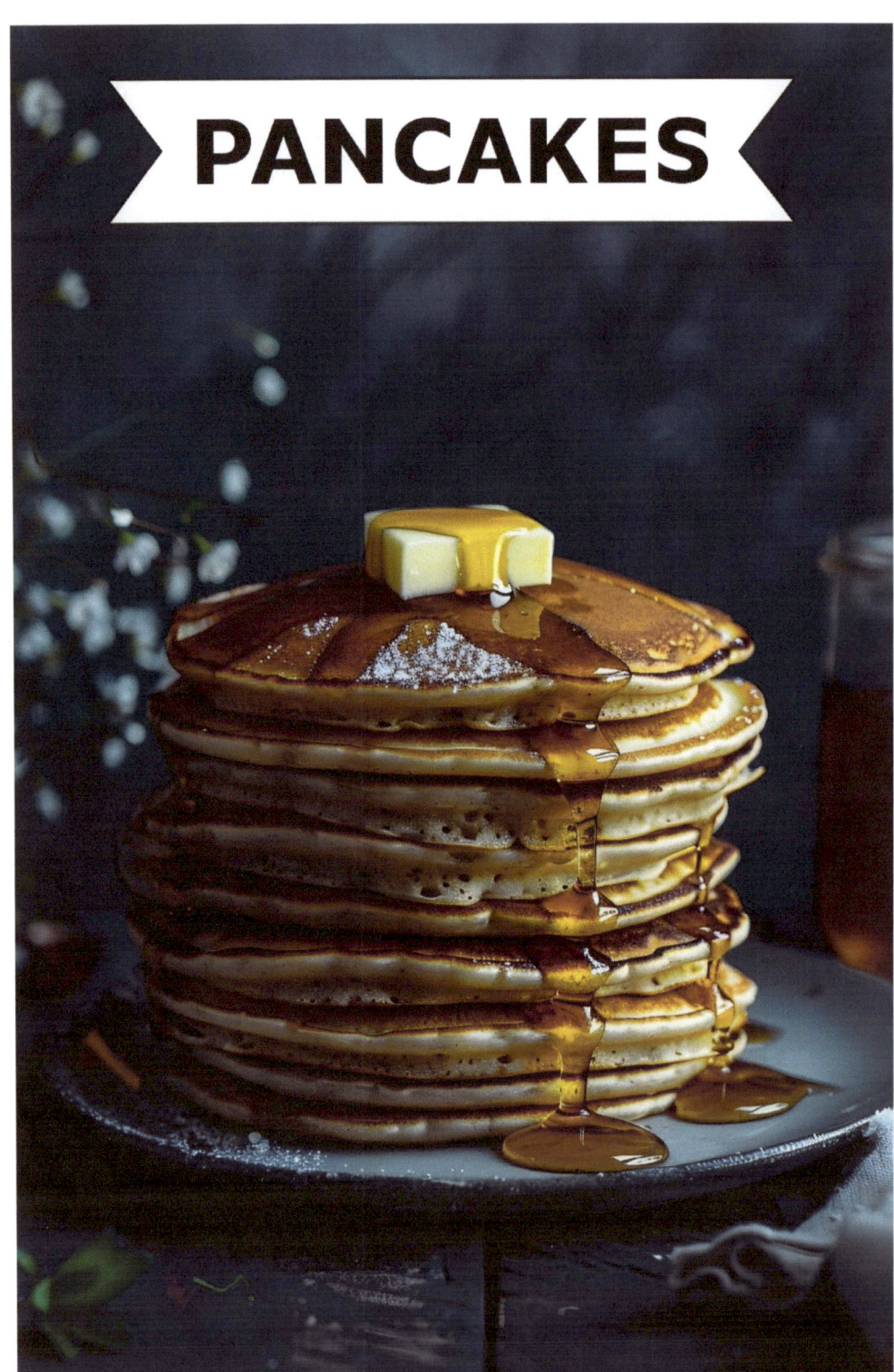

www.ingramcontent.com/pod-product-compliance
Lightning Source LLC
Chambersburg PA
CBHW040333220526
45473CB00009B/2673